At the Doorway

Eric Novak

For LeeAnna Studt,
who inspired this book
and continues to inspire me
every fucking day

Table of Contents

Acknowledgments

These are humans without who this book would have never made it off the shelves in my head:

LeeAnna Studt, Caitlin McManus, Kate Ford, Braden Poole, Ayethaw Tun, Karen Matkovitch, Denise & Dion Novak, Jonathan Castro, Eden & Al DeGenova, Jon Denny, Mary Erangey, Grant Daigle, Tracy & Mike Gutierrez, Marsha L. Hillson Gerace

An Explanation

I needed a job. I know, it's hard to believe that a college educated art student could have difficulty finding a job in this beautiful, blossoming economy, but whatever, that's beside the point. I applied for a job being a delivery driver at Papa John's Pizza. To my surprise/relief, I was hired shortly afterwards; however, I never knew such inspiration could spring from a job usually relegated by society as a haven for slackers, stoners, and other kinds of burnout losers. Well, a few weeks into the job, I was talking to LeeAnna Studt about some of the stranger deliveries I'd had so far and her constantly active brain hatched an idea: "Why don't you you write all these down and then illustrate them?"

Oh.

There's an idea. So, I set on creating all of the illustrations first. As I created the illustrations and wrote the poems, parts of me started to make their ways naturally into the poems and the artwork. Since each one was dependent on my memory of the person or the situation, I often found myself filling in the blanks with my own perceptions, which I had no idea of knowing whether they were even close to being accurate (in fact, they were probably way off). But that's kind of the point, isn't it? People are full of random, unsolicited judgments and the relationship between the customer and the delivery driver can be a precarious dance between what each party perceives and what is actually going on. So, I'm gonna be giving you a lot of potentially/probably false information, so just roll with it, ya know? Life is often full of misinformation and people are more often full of shit, myself included. This collection of experiences and people is a testament to human weirdness and the false perceptions that we so arrogantly bestow on people we don't even know. There were a few people here that I delivered to more than once, but for the most part, these deliveries were one time meetings and it's highly likely that I'll never see any of these people again. There's something beautiful in that; sharing a strange fleeting moment with a complete stranger, knowing that you'll never see them ever again. And all this shit happened at the doorway.

I. APARTMENTS

Yeah, I get it, fuck the tip, at least be weird

"Sorry I'm drunk"

Were her first words at the opening of the door

Two infants lay on the floor

Swaddled in faded rags atop their minuscule beds

To the mundanity of apartment living

She fumbled with the receipt as I fumbled with my thoughts

Did these babies care

If their mother was a drunk fool?

Was that even fair

For me to say?

But these thoughts were fleeting

As the door moaned in closing

Later my phone chimed in its usual discord

"Who is this?"

Words from a mother inebriated and full

Of cheese

And regret?

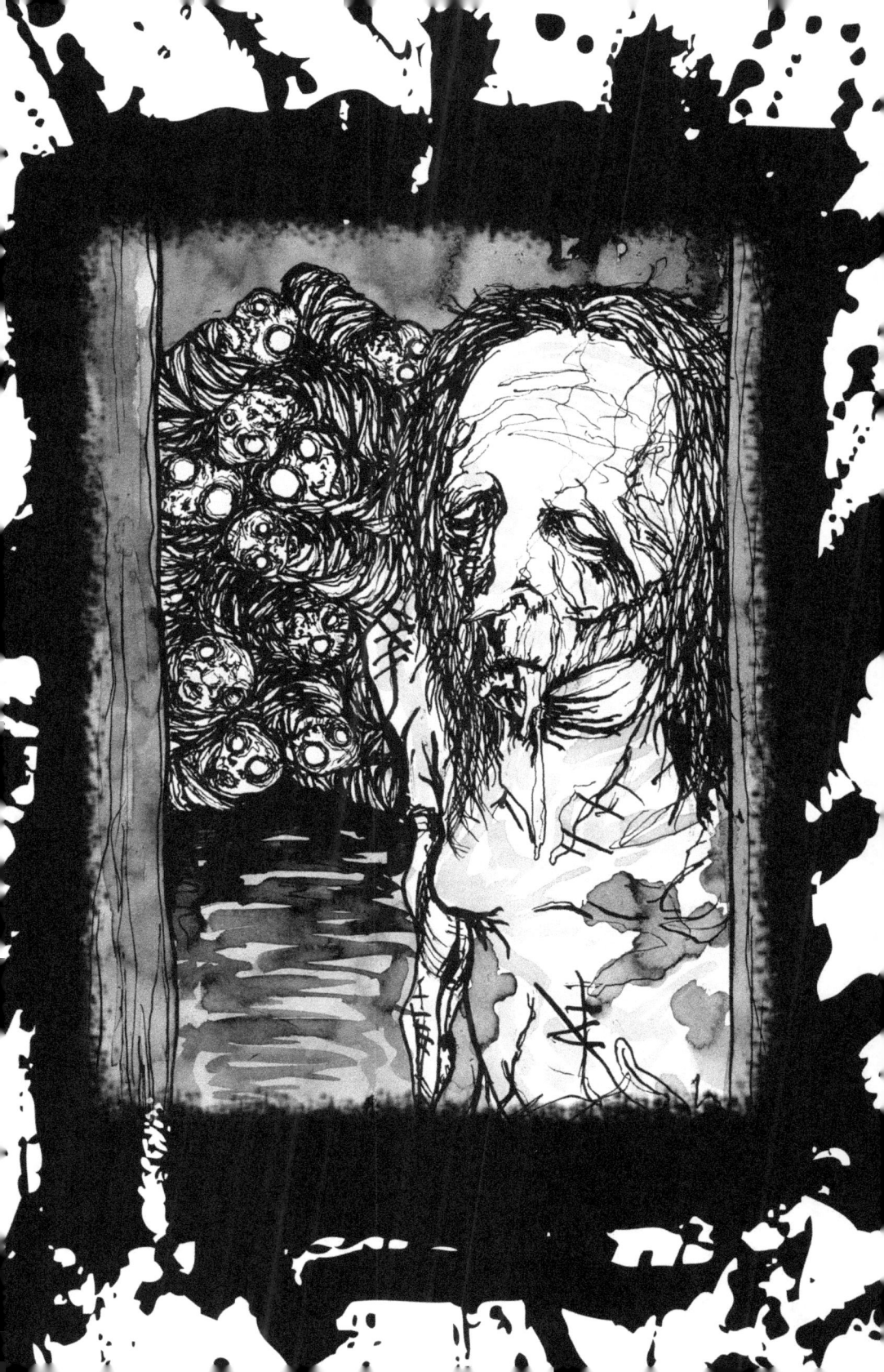

A torn sleeve

Distracts from a tattered brow

And how

His face is a wrinkled sheet

Of paranoia and pain

As he feigns a look of delight

Exits for a moment

To sign the receipt

And silence

A silence that shrouds

Past anguish

Or future evil

It threatens to envelop

Until the crumpled scrap of paper

Is thrust forward

Torn slightly

And simultaneously

Silence shredded

By the slamming of the door

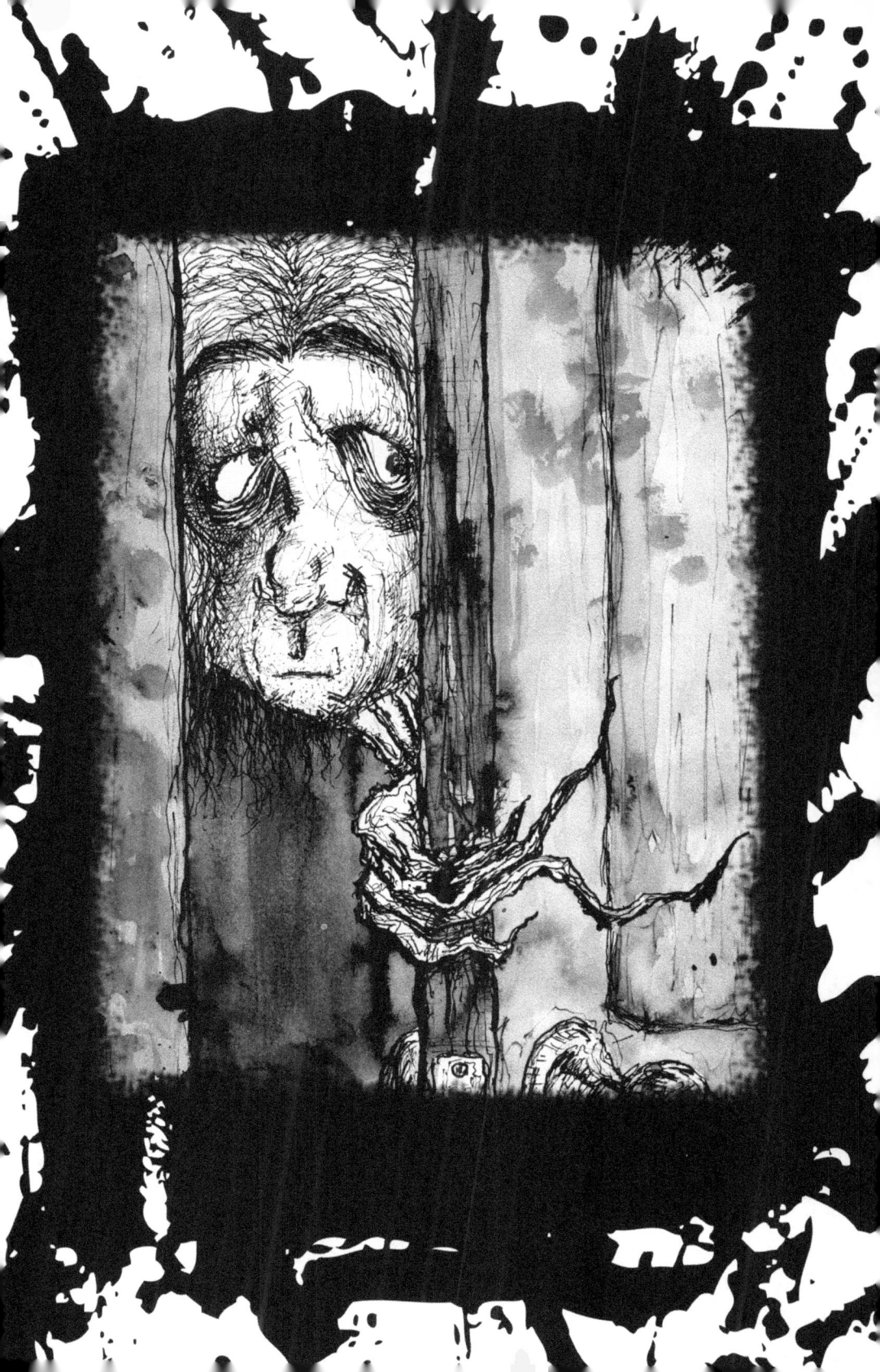

Close to home base

1303 Hershey Place

A sleek black limousine lay bloated in the driveway

Piloted by an elaborately embellished man

Suit giving off a dull twinkle

In the light of the weary moon

A woman walks out

Fiercely elevated

By more than portable purple stilts

Followed by the dull click

Of cheap plastic on cracked cement

Until she waits behind me

As I rap against the wood of the door

The man had a face sculpted by Jack Daniel himself

And as he struggled to keep his jaw from falling from his face

I struggled to give him his pizza

As I could have sworn

Glitter began to litter the back of my neck

I turned away

As the man slurred and struggled

With his pizza and pants

While a child no older than five

Watched from behind the corner

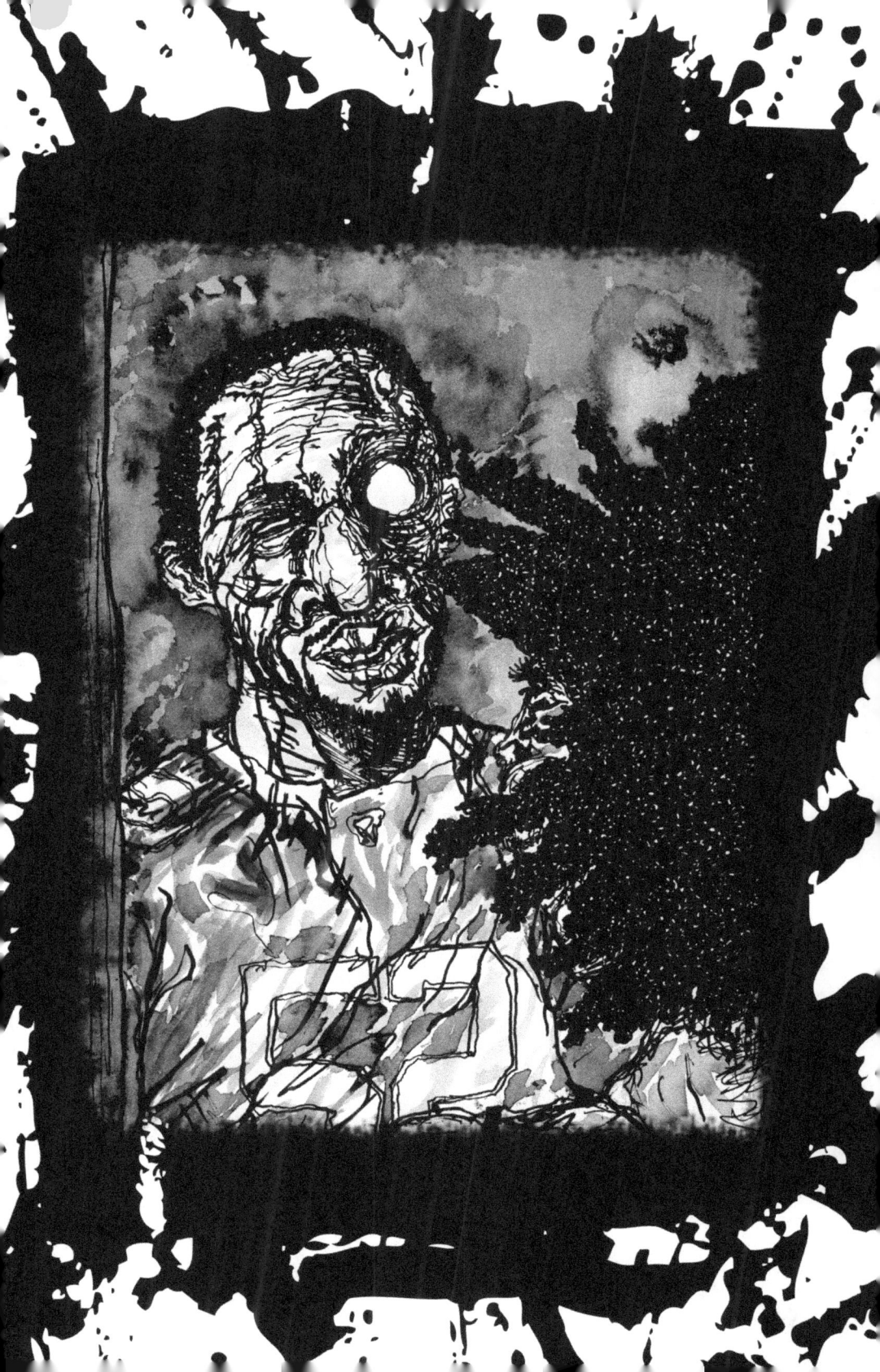

A dream of thumping 70's grooves

Was muffled

Pushing against the moaning fibers of the door

Until my knock forbid it from further action

Answered by a plum and an asparagus

Eyes glued to each other in savage desire

The man's shirt ripped open in a deep V

A musk coated the air

Air rippling with a hot moisture

Record player frozen on the back shelf

As if playing red light green light

And green light made it glad

Thanking the gods of vinyl

That they grant it only the powers

To seduce the ear

While those with the gift of sight

Moaned in protest

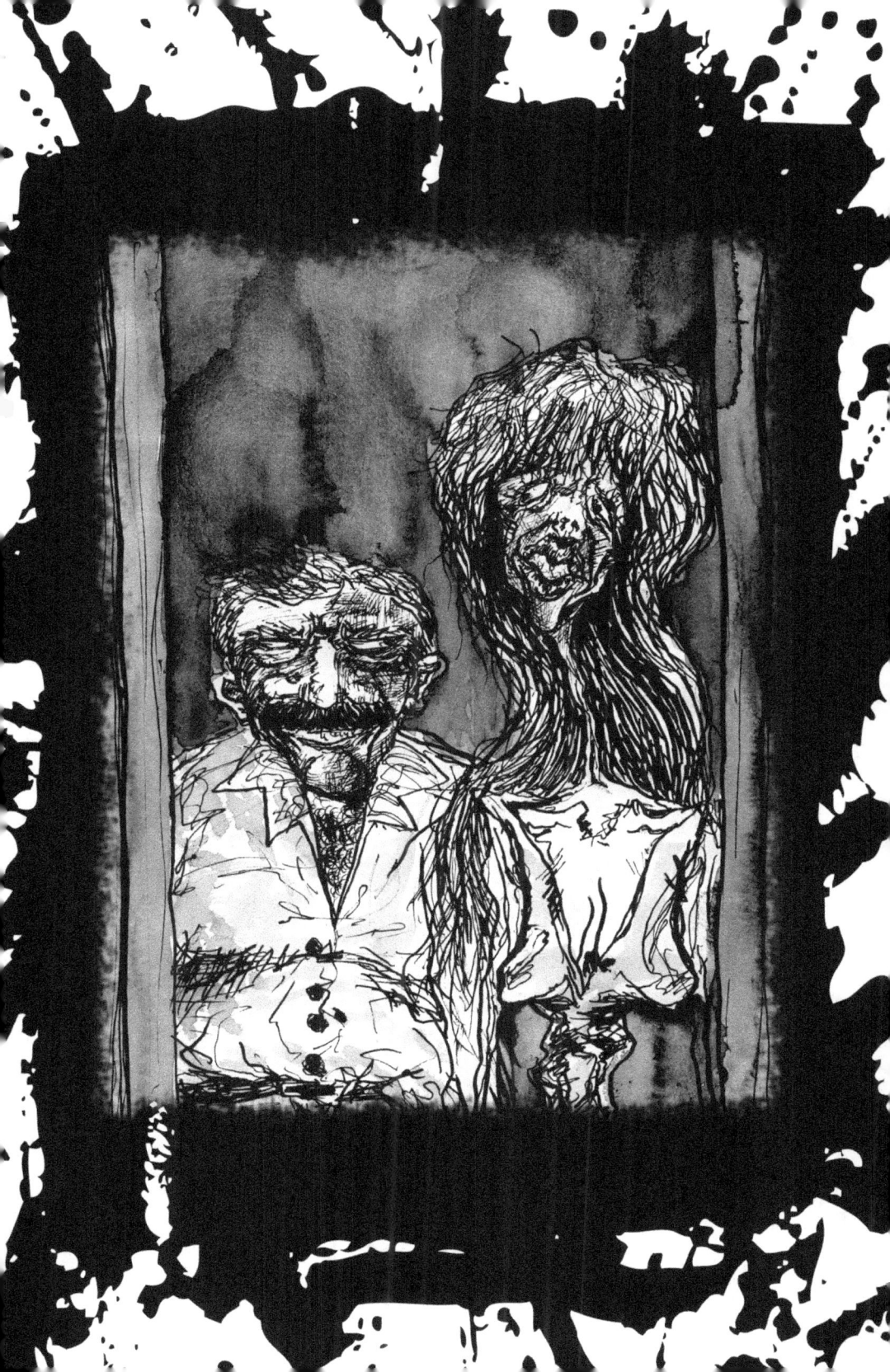

Rudder Lane

Land of the sprained ankle

A disturbance!

In the tallest room

Of the tallest tower

By the pizza man

Streamers!

A cake!

Friends! (...as far as I knew)

These should have been tell tale signs!

Had I only known

Before the knock

With the ritual interrupted

He may never break on through

To the other side

I guess the spirit of Rudder never really left me alone

From then on

Until it had its petty revenge

Months later

A sprained ankle

And a temporary release

From this godforsaken place

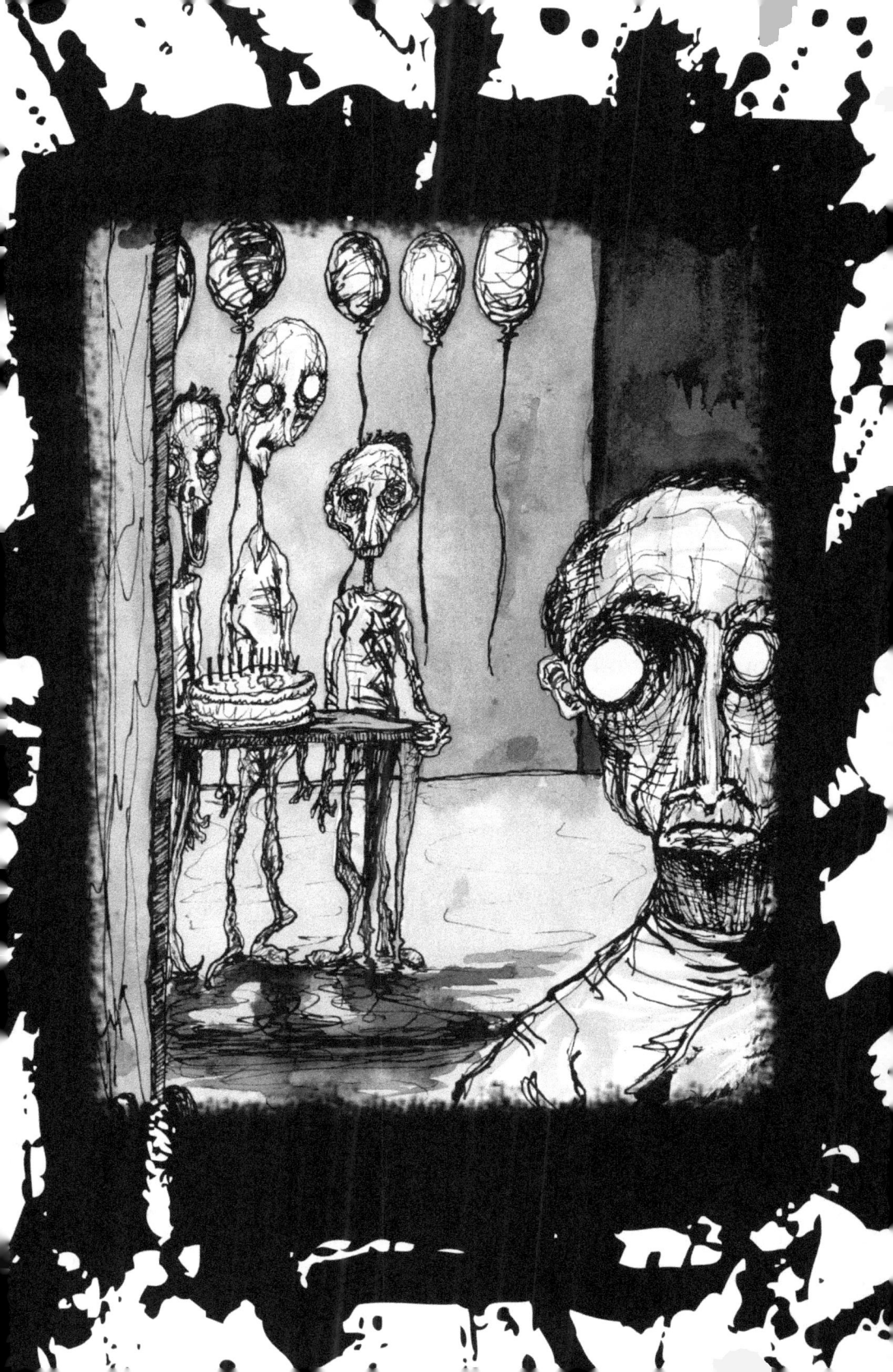

"Send a cute delivery boy"

Chuckle replaced by facetious questioning

"Hey James, am I cute enough for this?"

Approval sends my self-esteem racing down Veterans Parkway

Past cops and crashes

Straight to Peirce Avenue

A man opens the door

Shedding light on the darkness

Lips drawn into an obvious frown

Only interpreted as disgust

Acting as Truman's hand

To the Hiroshima of my confidence

Empty wine bottles hung slightly askew

From frames easily bought from Hobby Lobby

Back at the store

Phone rings

"Can you send a cuter delivery boy this time?"

Rang his words, verbally this time

"We're all pretty much the same cuteness around here"

A grunt

A dial tone

Then laughter

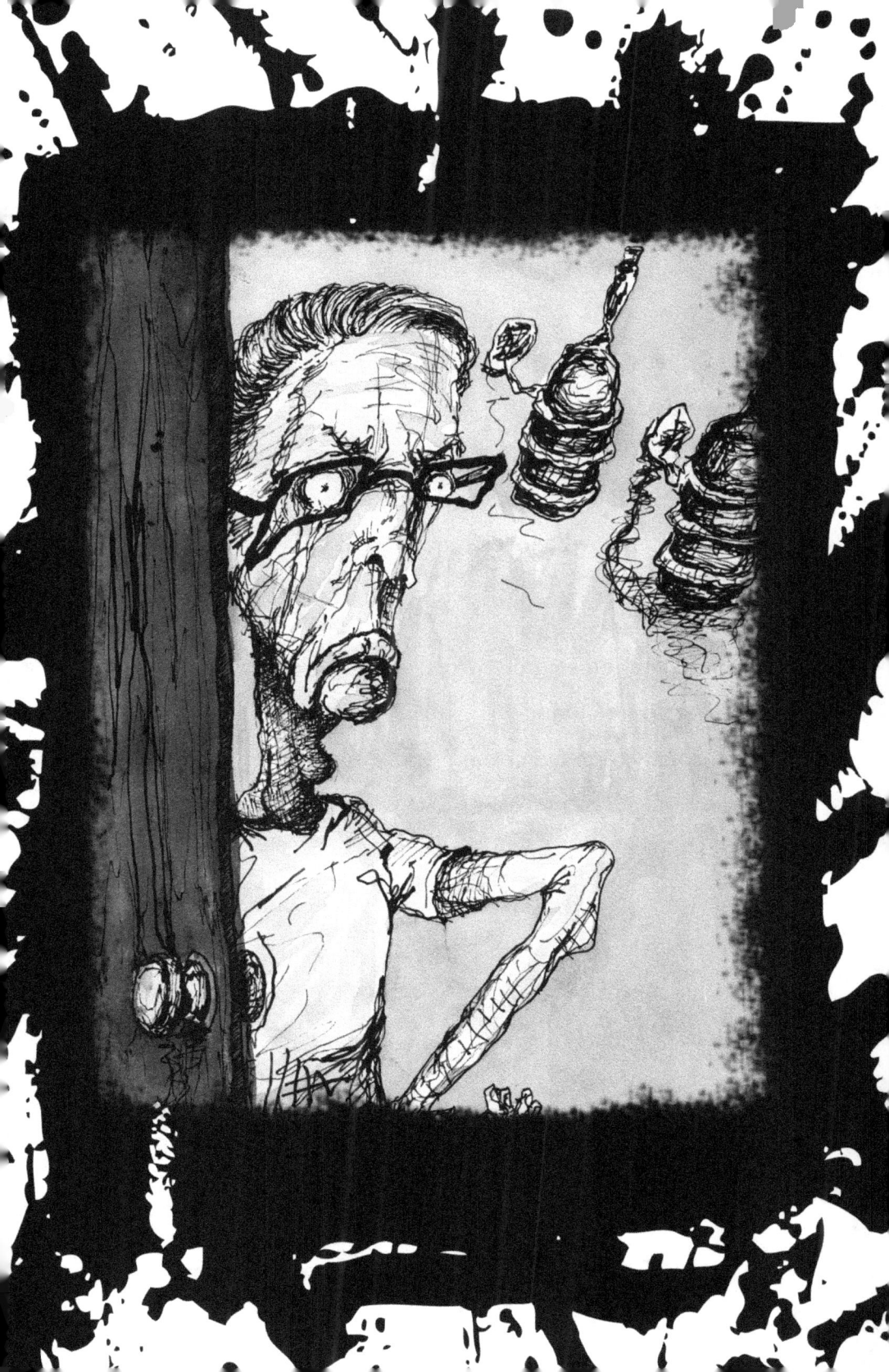

Like an aborted terrace

I climbed up knotted steps

Like stepping on the toes of grandmother

The squeaked, but only barely

The apartment was at the very end

A tossed aside affair

A dusty woman answered the door

Her eyes bulging

Engorged meatballs

Juices slipping silently from each puncta

Her pupils threatened to overthrow the color
in her eyes

I knew that look

Confusing color and sound

As new avenues are found

By the normally dormant corners of the mind

But this wasn't a look of fearless discovery

This was a look of pure horror

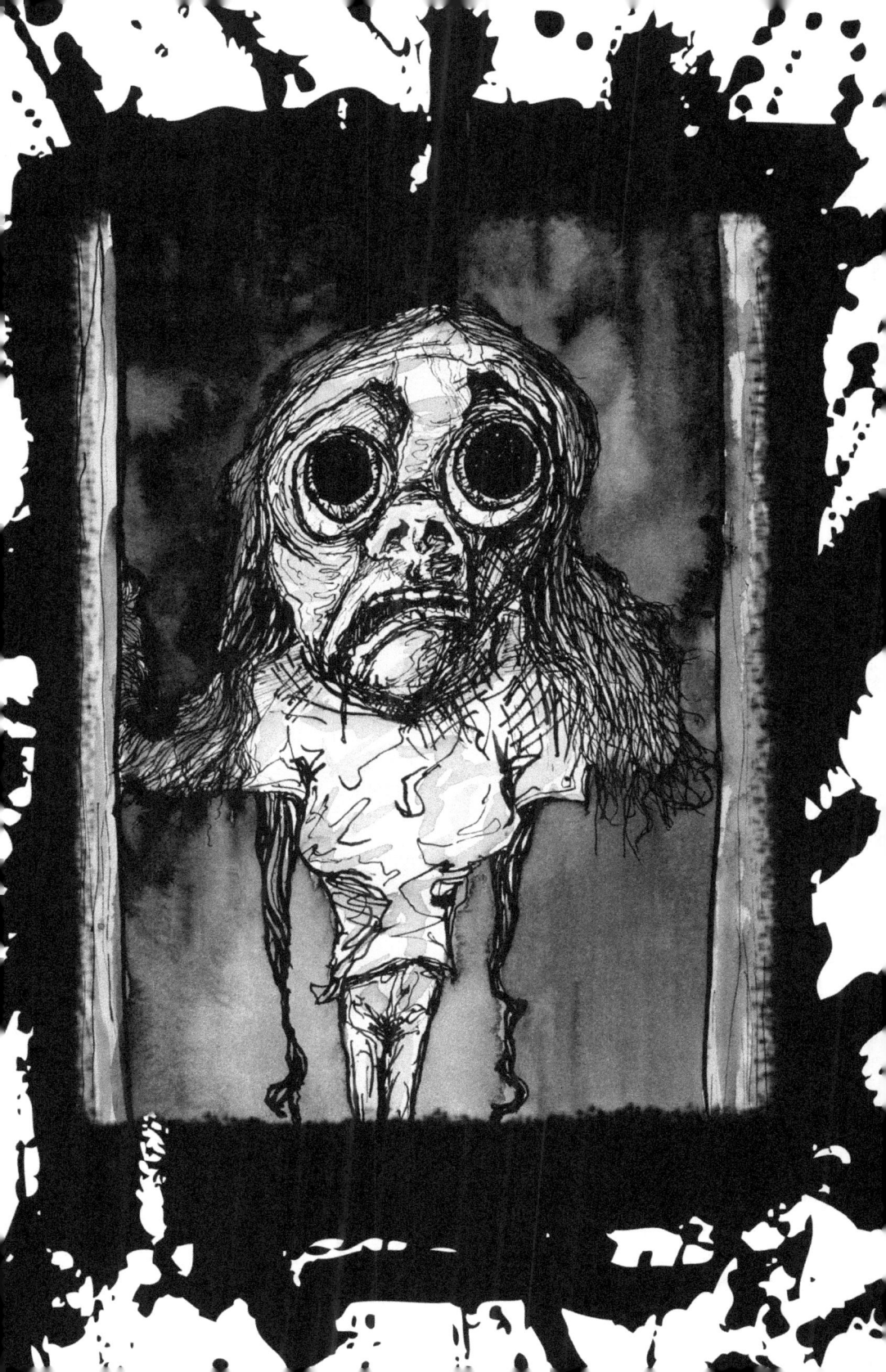

The walls of this shithole were unassuming.

Content to remain in the background

Giving and taking nothing

Perhaps in fear of the strange man standing before me

Eyes as two extraterrestrial saucers

Fallen over the craggy hills of his grin

Which was perched on his face like a bloated magpie

He stood a little higher than a tree stump

Although built like a robust twig

Hand grasped the marker with tenuous certainty

As the ink filtered through the membrane of the wax

...Long after the sealing of the his home

Did I realize the latency of his larceny

My marker was gone

Abducted by his own Area 51

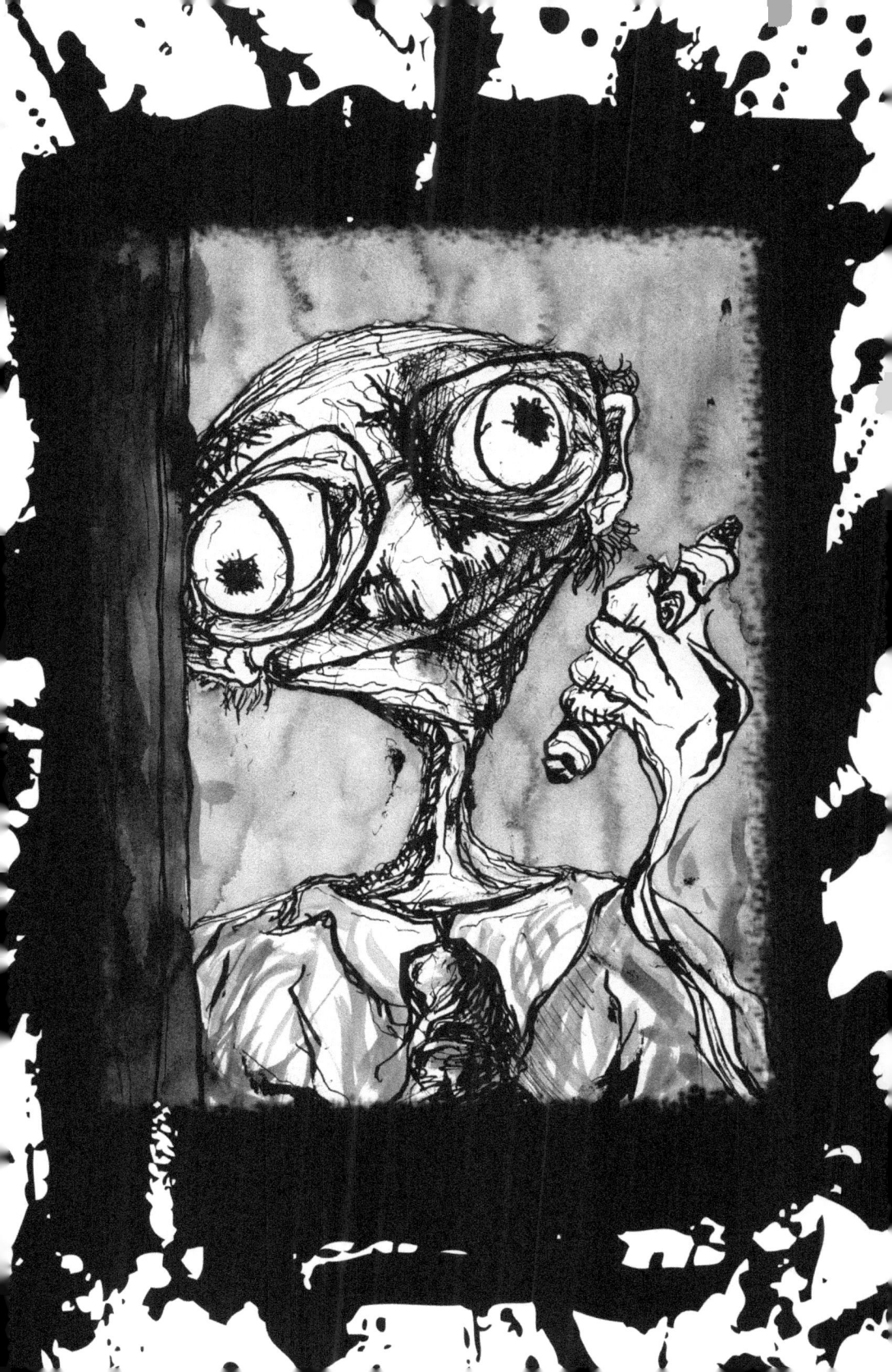

"doesn't know address

behind normal theater"

Ovens overheated

As car engines reheat

Bright Vegas strip glow of the Normal Theater

Stops me in my tracks

"Aw no, dude, I'm behind the other movie theater"

A comical redness fell over the top of my head

As the light walked to the back of my window

Across town to a theatre

Lit by the small town carnival glow of a small
town carnival

Hiding a small cluster of houses

Clothed in brick

Until a cartoonishly noir light

Hanging over the head of a used cigarette butt

Slack jaw cradling a bent white cylinder

Smoking and attempting to mask

The fucking stupid look plastered on his face

Sheepishly took the pizza

Murmuring something

That could have been an apology

But who cares?

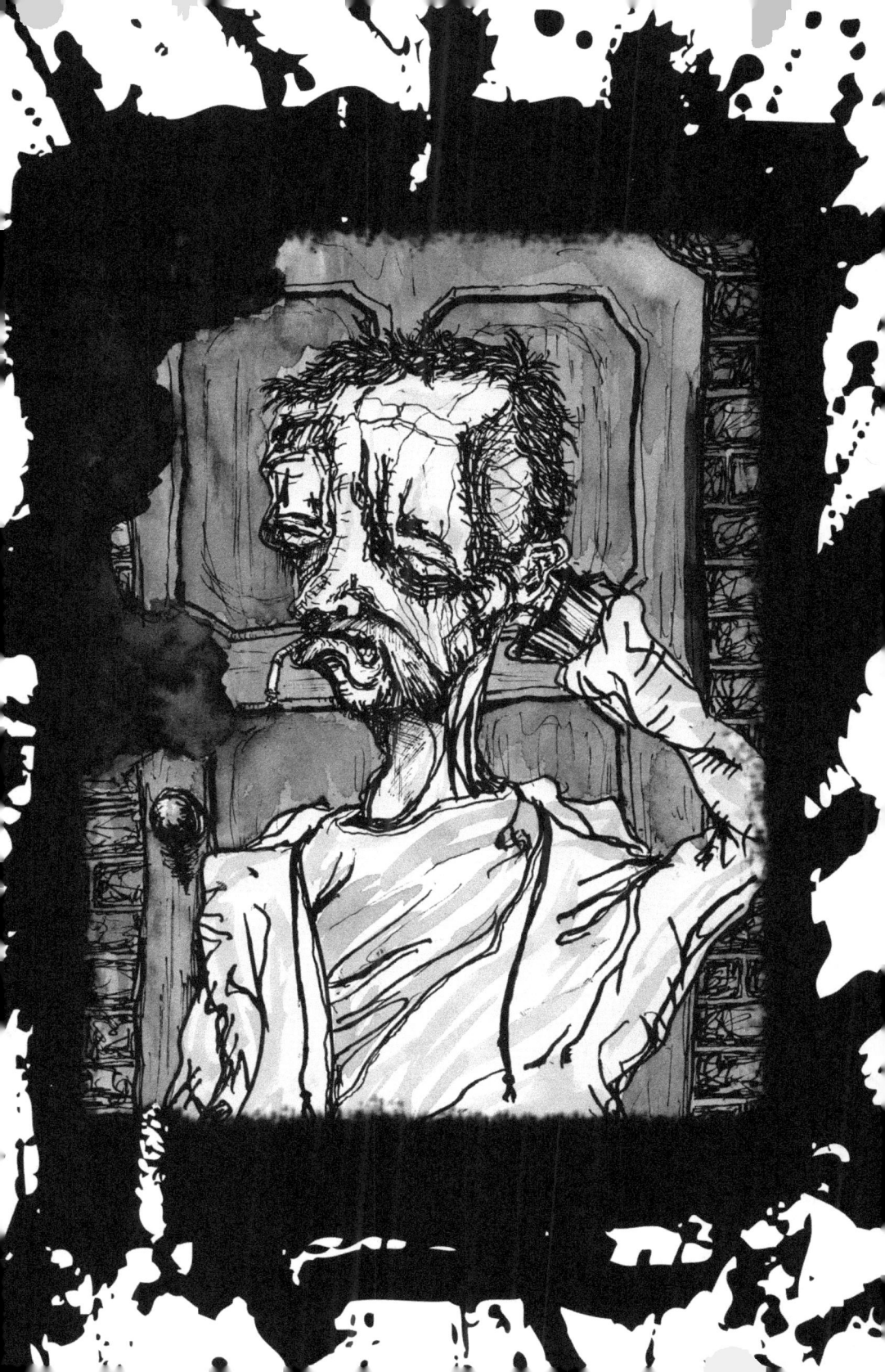

Clone Crushers

Salt Slashers

Power Punch

Some damn phone game

Apparently engrossing to the point

Of total envelopment

Mundane tasks like signing for a pizza

Become invisible

As the body carries out in instinctual motion

That which is necessary

To get me to leave

A woman slides up to the door

Friction between her legs completely

Unnoticeable

Croons lavender language into his ear

Somehow shattering

His technological shield

He looks up

Signs the receipt

Shuts the door

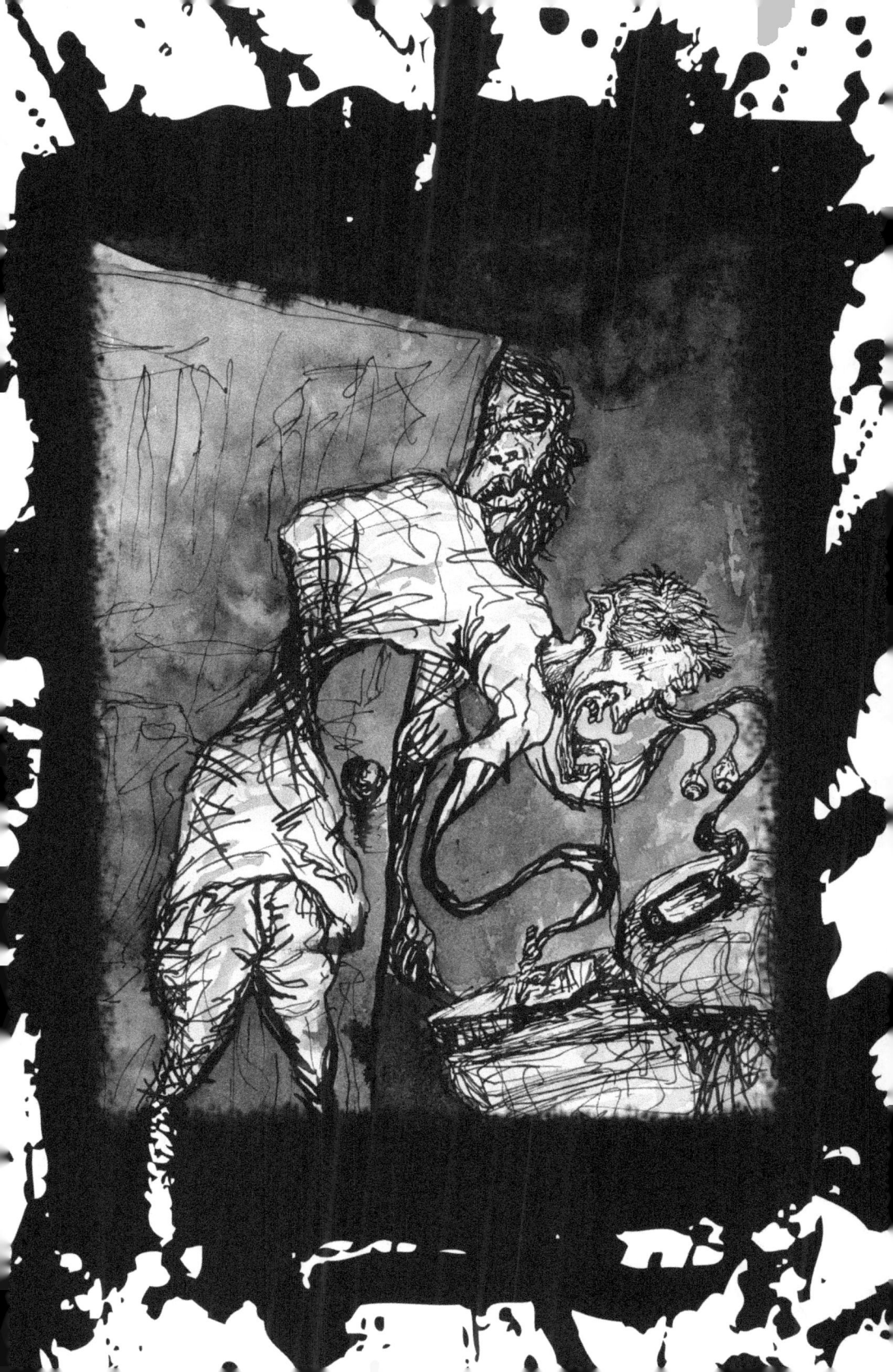

The familiar knock

With the familiar suspension of sound

A dull shuffle

Muffled words scratch at the door

As the lock fumbles for its purpose

The door opens and the room exhales

A long exasperated sigh

Then invasion by an alien odor

Becomes all that is

Shit stacked like books

And books piled like shit

Cover the carpet in a labyrinth

Occupied by cats and the stench of the 70s

And just below eye level

Stands a wobbly woman

Tethered to earth by some unknown force

She speaks a petite squeak

Which highlights a bristled mouth

And two ivory teeth peek from within

Interlocking like pieces of a puzzle

Suddenly the smell evacuates

And left staring at the receipt

Which mockingly reads at the closing of the door

"Tip: $0.24"

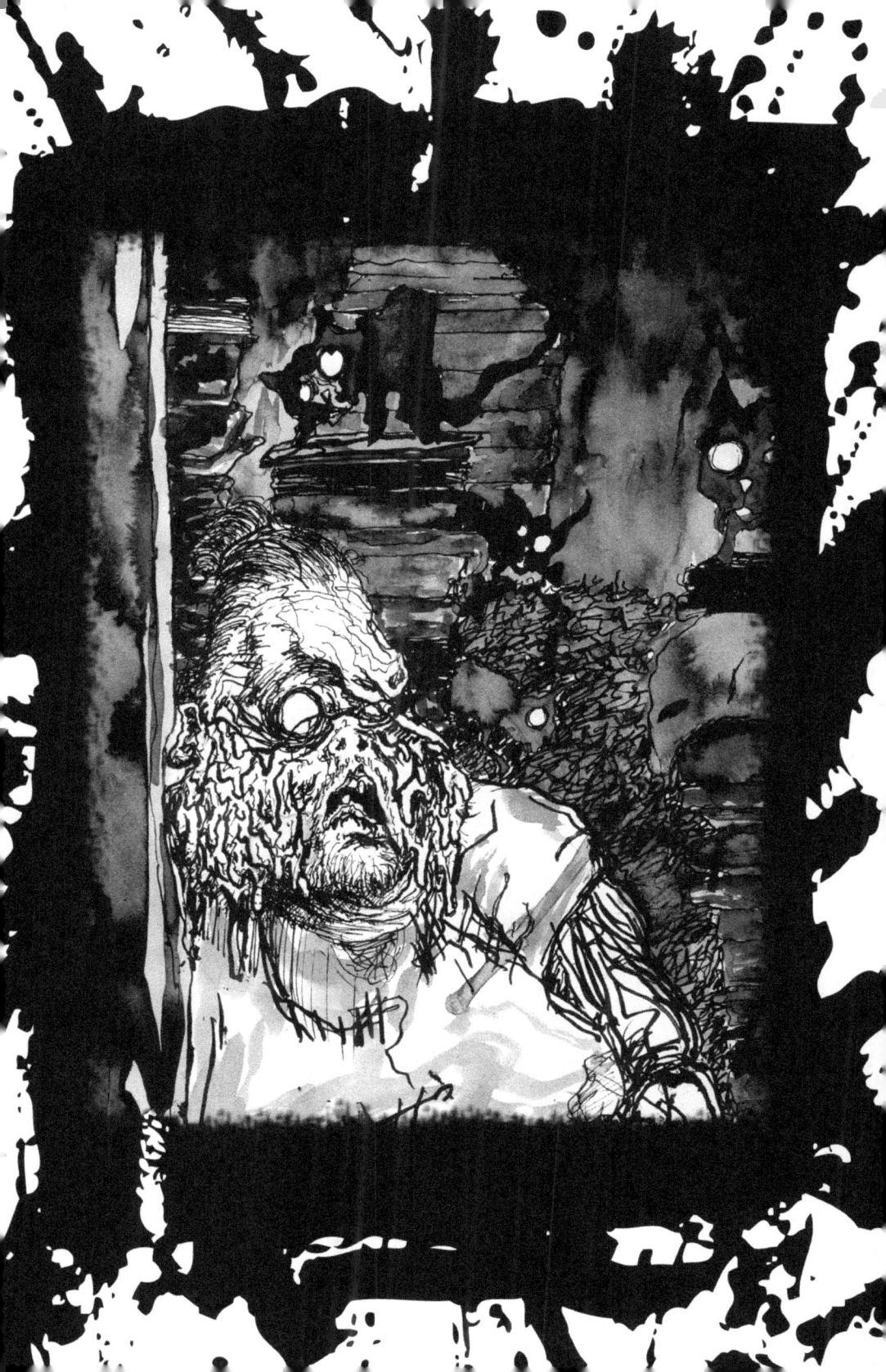

Out of another foolishly laid out apartment building

Stumbles Jerry Seinfeld

As if he had been committed

Instead of finding fame

He became a recluse and a basket case

Faced with bitter loneliness

No George Costanza to share

Instead paired with a cat

And that's that

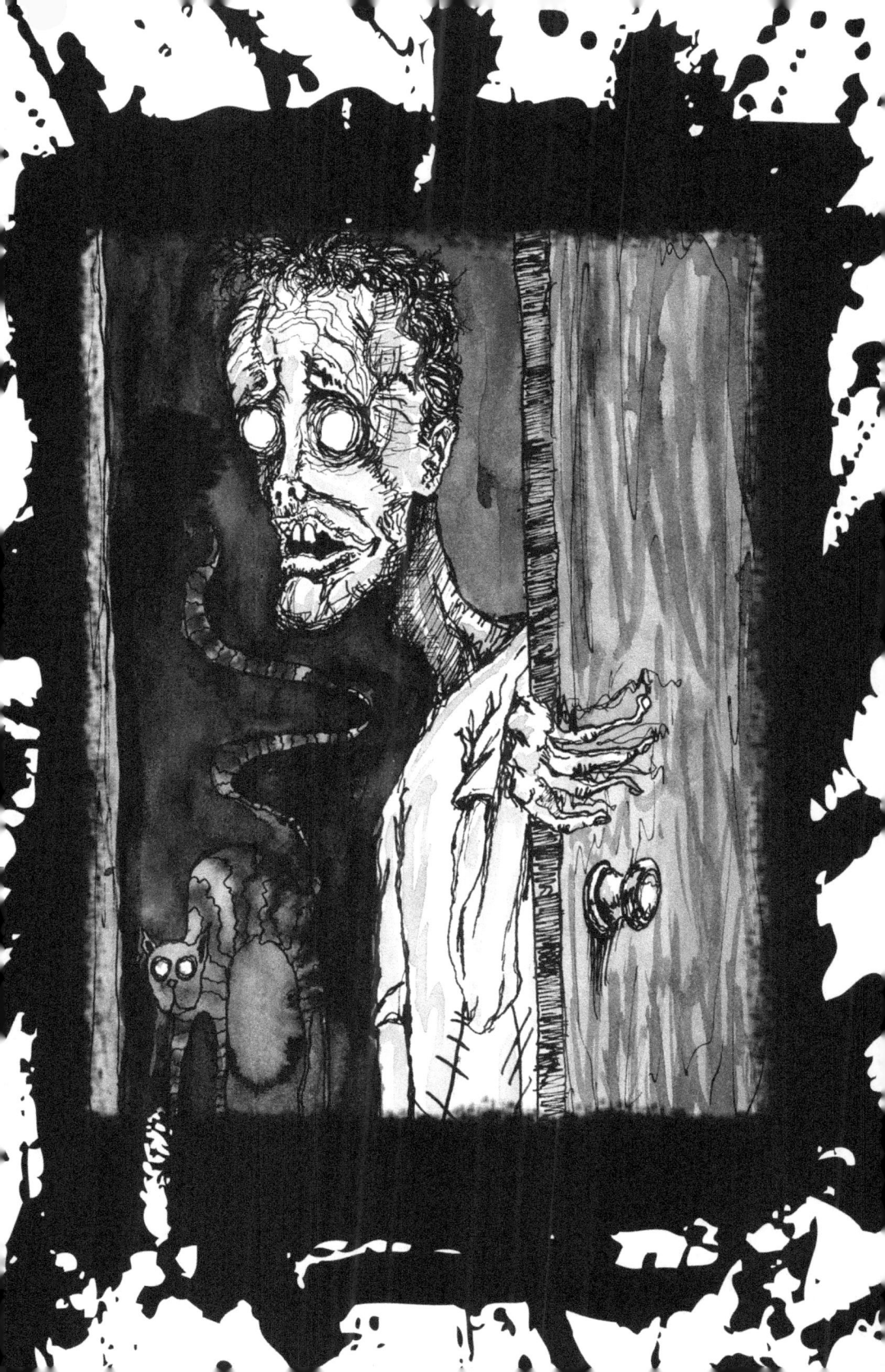

2:34 a.m.--

Washington apartments--

Final delivery of the night...

Several unrequited knocks

Suddenly the cries of children at play!

A circling of the apartment

No bodies, yet voices floated through the air

Like afterbirth in the bath

And knocks yielded nothing

--Zooming out--

From across the street, skeptically watching

A shirtless rail of a man and a scraggled feline

Walking slowly as if knowledgeable

Of spirits and lost ones beyond the unassuming door

Emblazoned with the rusted number six

As I walked away, the screams of the children

Gradually faded into the wind of the morning

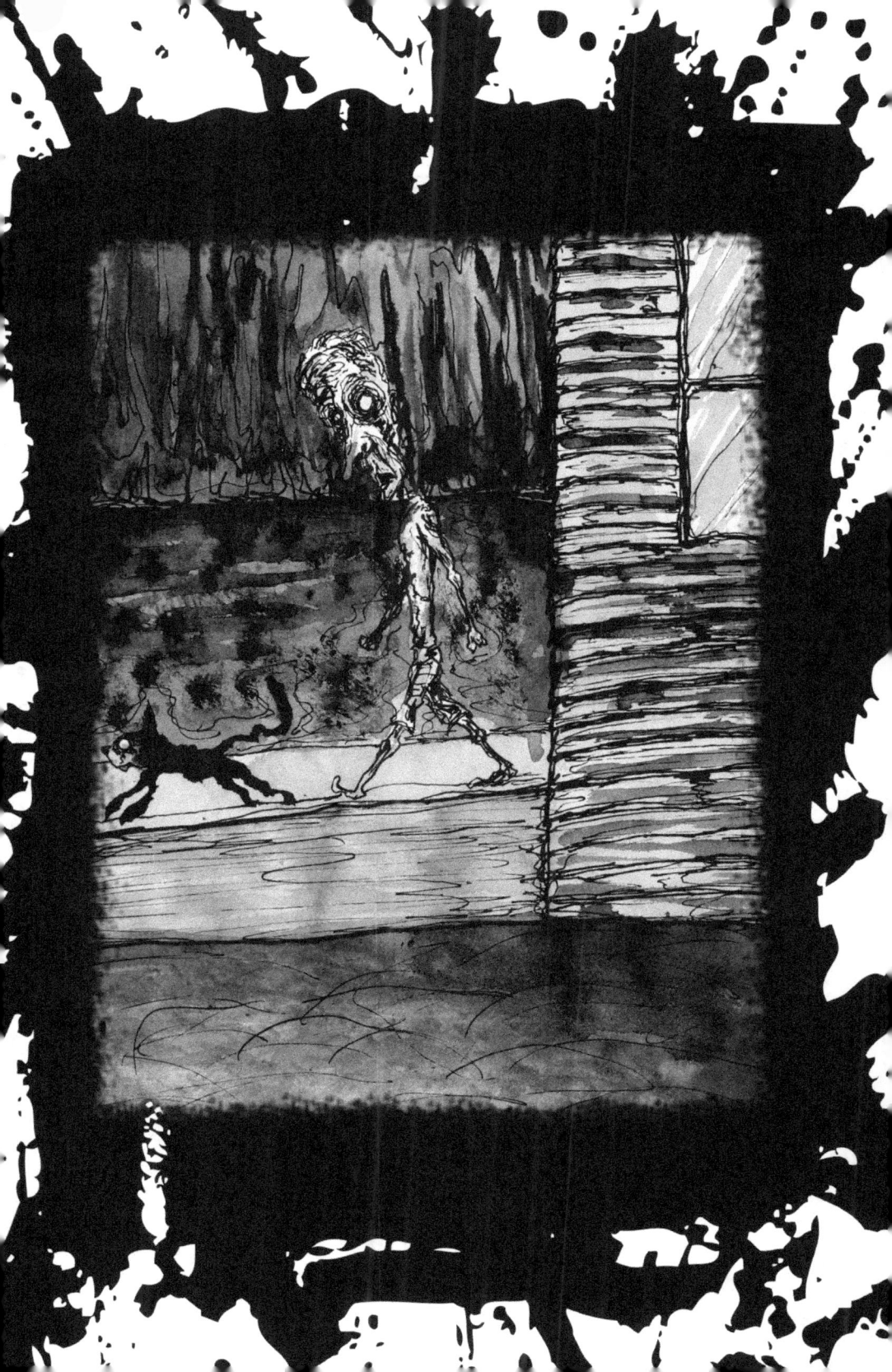

It was a cat suit

A fucking cat suit

And a guy with an afro like Gil Scott Heron

Like some anime characters

I guess they need a place to live too

From all of the fully rendered

Fleshy 3-D models

Of the natural world

They didn't say anything

Worth remembering

Focusing all of their memorability

On what I saw before me

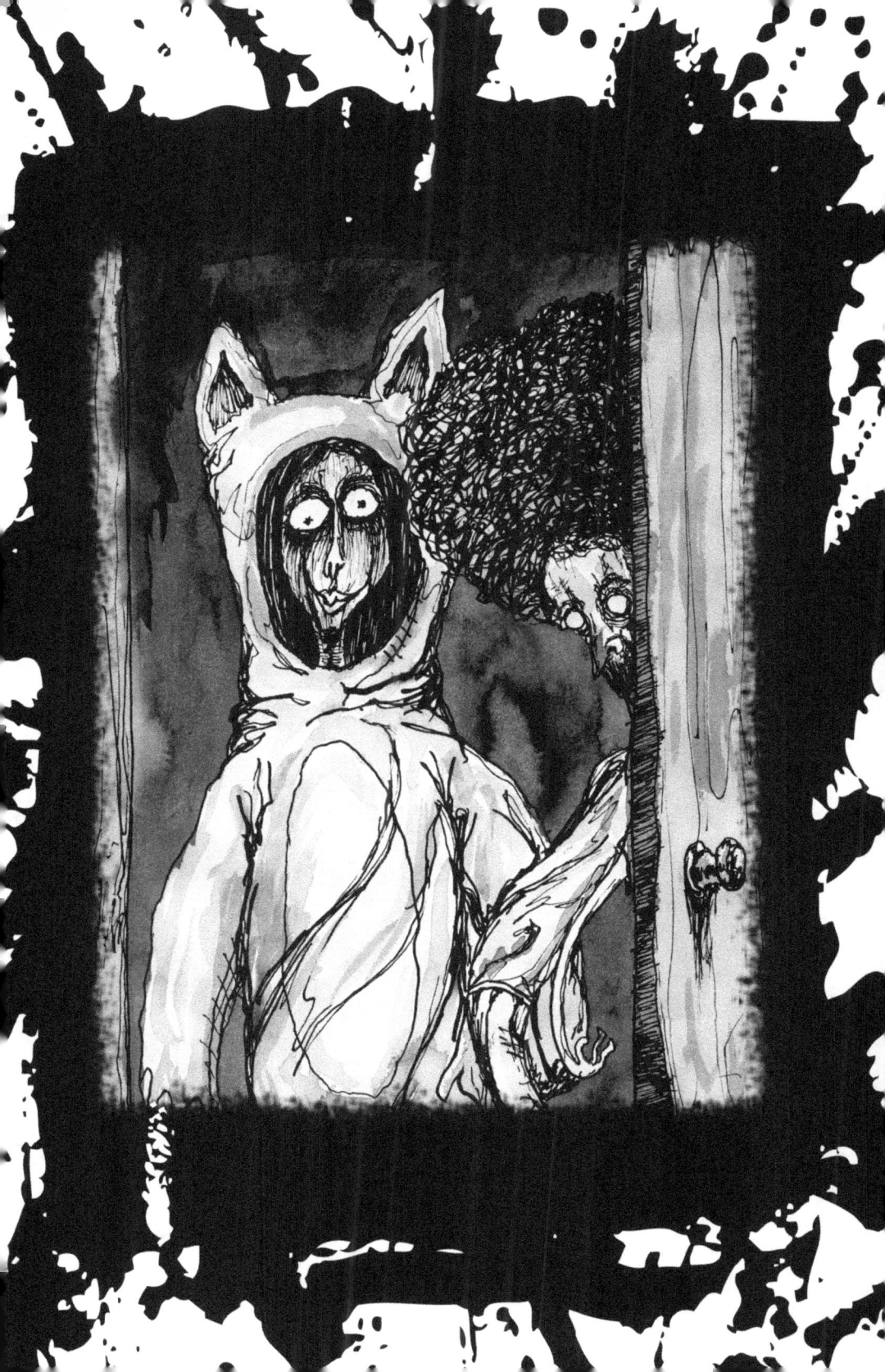

Slathered

By the leather of a tongue

Leaving behind a glistening field

Of salivary secretion

Was yanked back

By naked nails

The dog's floppy grin remaining steadfast

"She always does this..."

In reference to the dog's daring escape plan

Nails clenching the collar

She always tries to escape?

What kind of fucked up family was this?

That such a pleasant dog

Could be pleading for help so desperately

A rusting cage was just behind

A man leaning like a surfboard

Glared from just over the top of the dog

A stare sinister as can be

In such an environment

Whispering

"Don't you say a damn word

This is not your business"

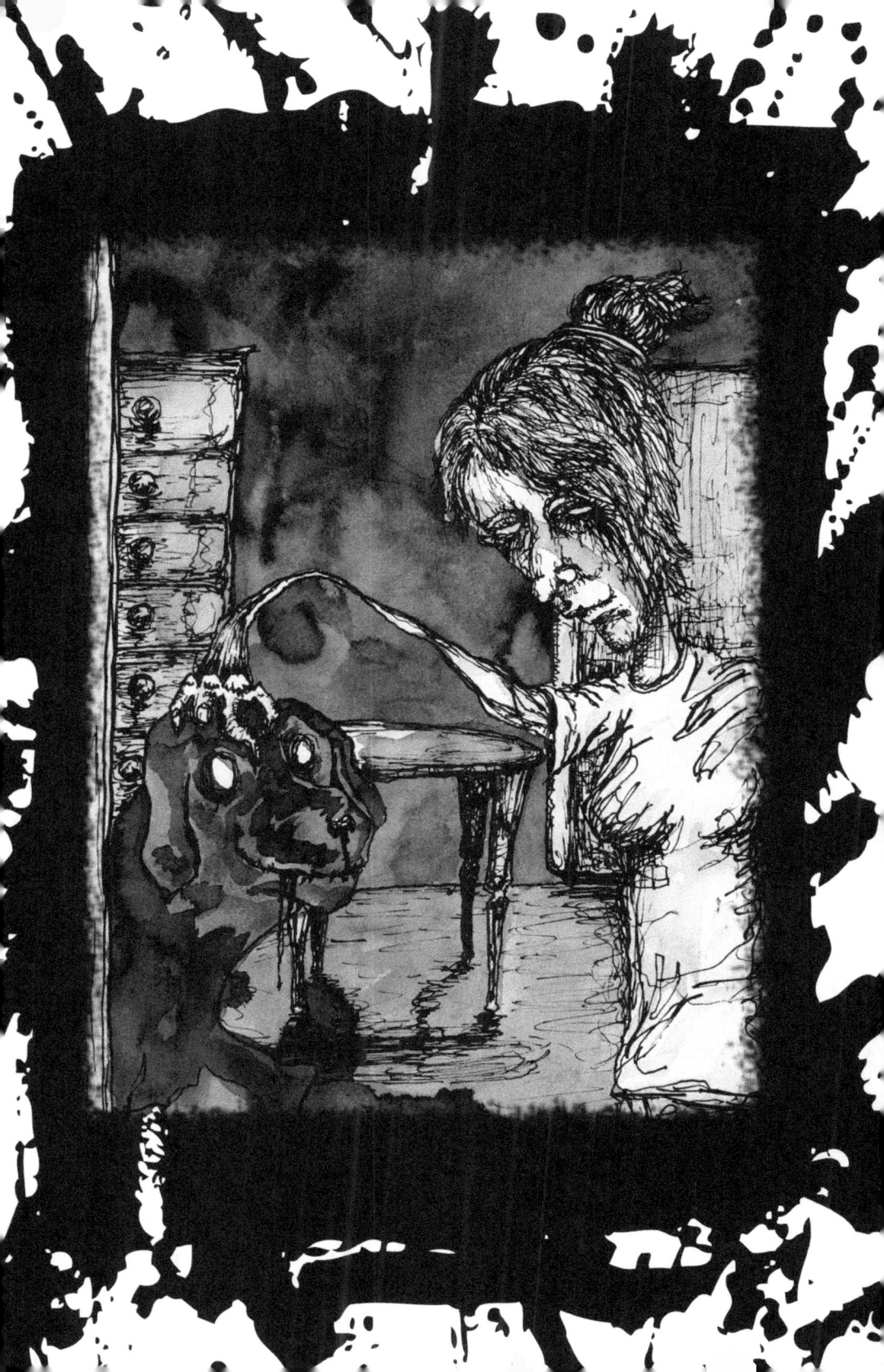

The door springs away

From the gnarled flesh of my fist

And betrays an apartment threatening

To collapse in on itself-

Clad in rags and regret

A woman rasps a demand

From her gray upholstered throne

A man with a neck like a twig

And a head like an aged scrotum

Manages to croak out a word

Before being drowned out

By two scrappy dogs

Suffering from Napoleon complex

The woman's incessant cawing

Peeling off the air like old wallpaper

Coupled with the man's placid grin

Brought thoughts of what might've been

Had their lives gone separate ways

The dogs kept their distance

But gave countless barking barbs

As if their yips and yaps

Will lead me to snap

And bolt into the day

My tail quivering between my legs

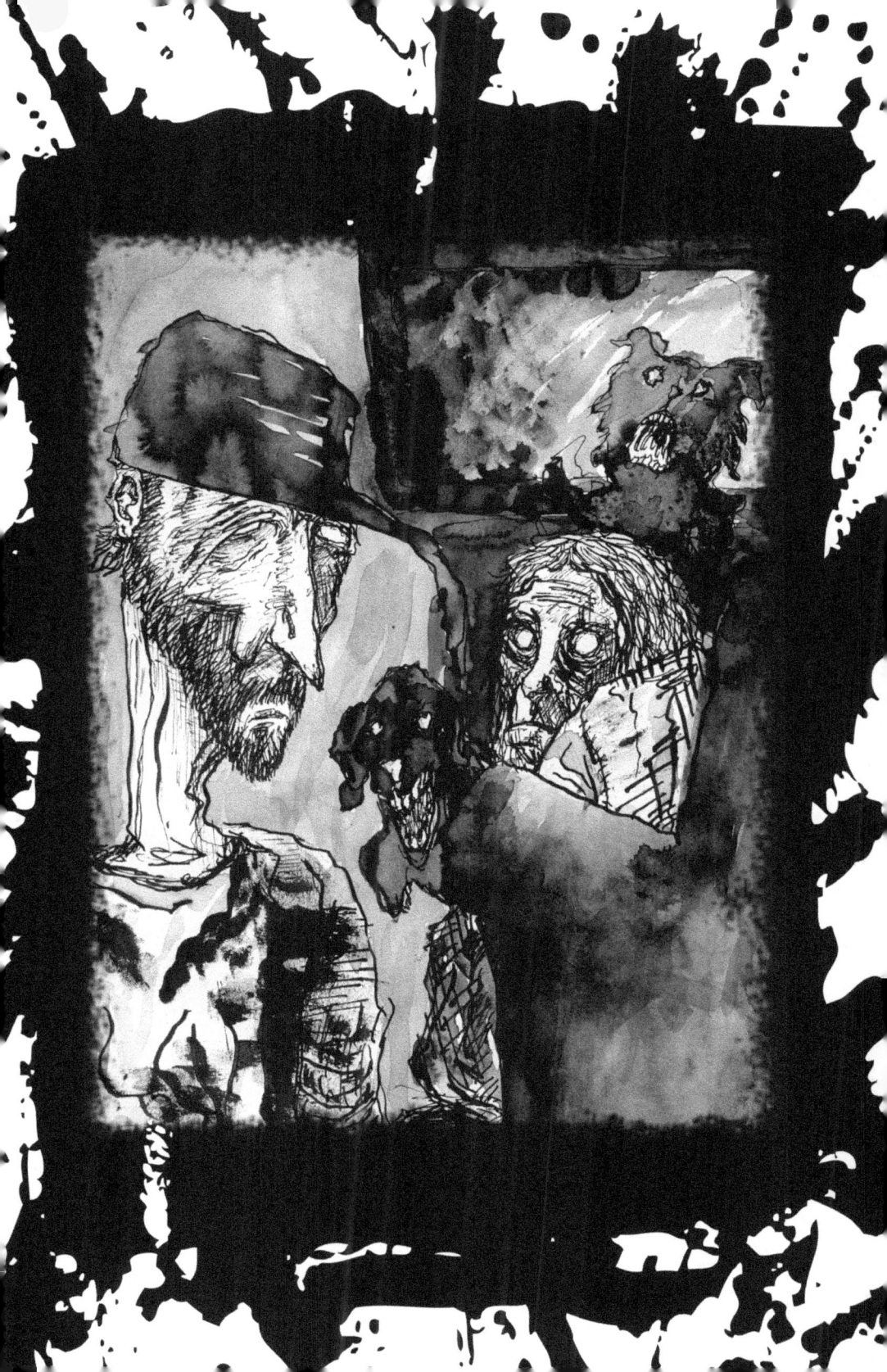

Oh boy

The house itself was riddled with pockmarks

Narrowly dodging a dive bombing shingle

Its kamikaze strike barely failing

Ignored by a muttering man, slumped on the front step

Accompanied by a dog like a burnt french fry

Suddenly a smack and a yelp jumped up behind me

As the door slowly opened

A legless woman rolls out

Rusted wheelchair barely together

Her eyes careening in every direction

The man's muttering continued

In spite of the woman's stilted speech

As a small child crawled away with the pizza

And an eye fell at last on me

"Goodbye"

She managed to croak as the door closed

The simple movement threatening

The entire foundation of the house

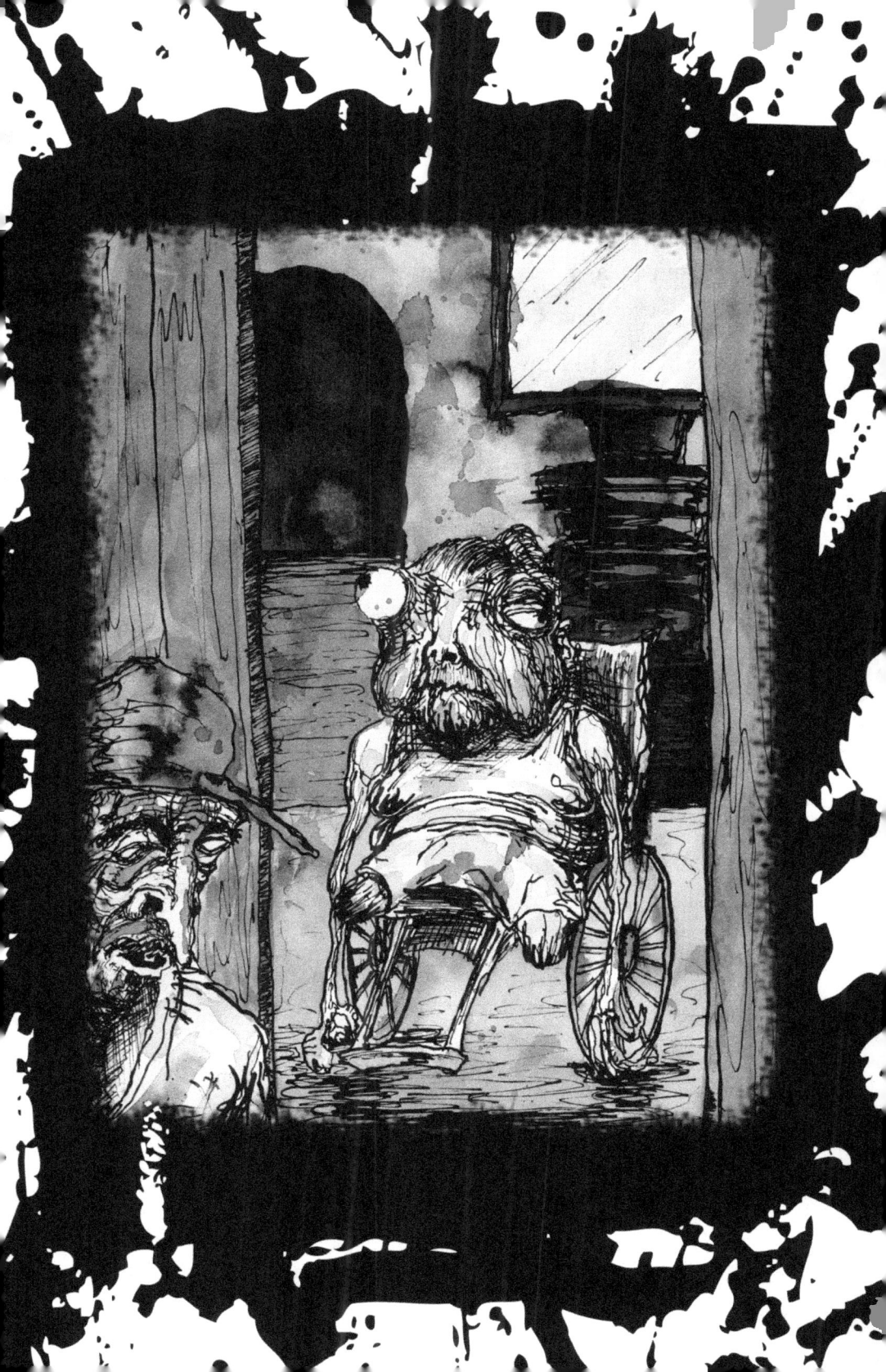

One house stretched

By the clumsy hands of a giant

Gingerly, without splitting

Into three separate homes

The woman who answered the center door

Was young

With eyes blazing like the heart of a volcano

Greeted me with hair encircling an orbiting smile

Landing on every inch

Of our surrounding atmosphere

Her voice firing like a haywire machine gun

Hitting every inch

Of my susceptible psyche

A hastily assembled playdough child

Sort of puttered around

On the sleek tile of the floor

Back to her omnipresent grin

Unchanged this whole time

Eyes falling meteors

At the collapse of the door

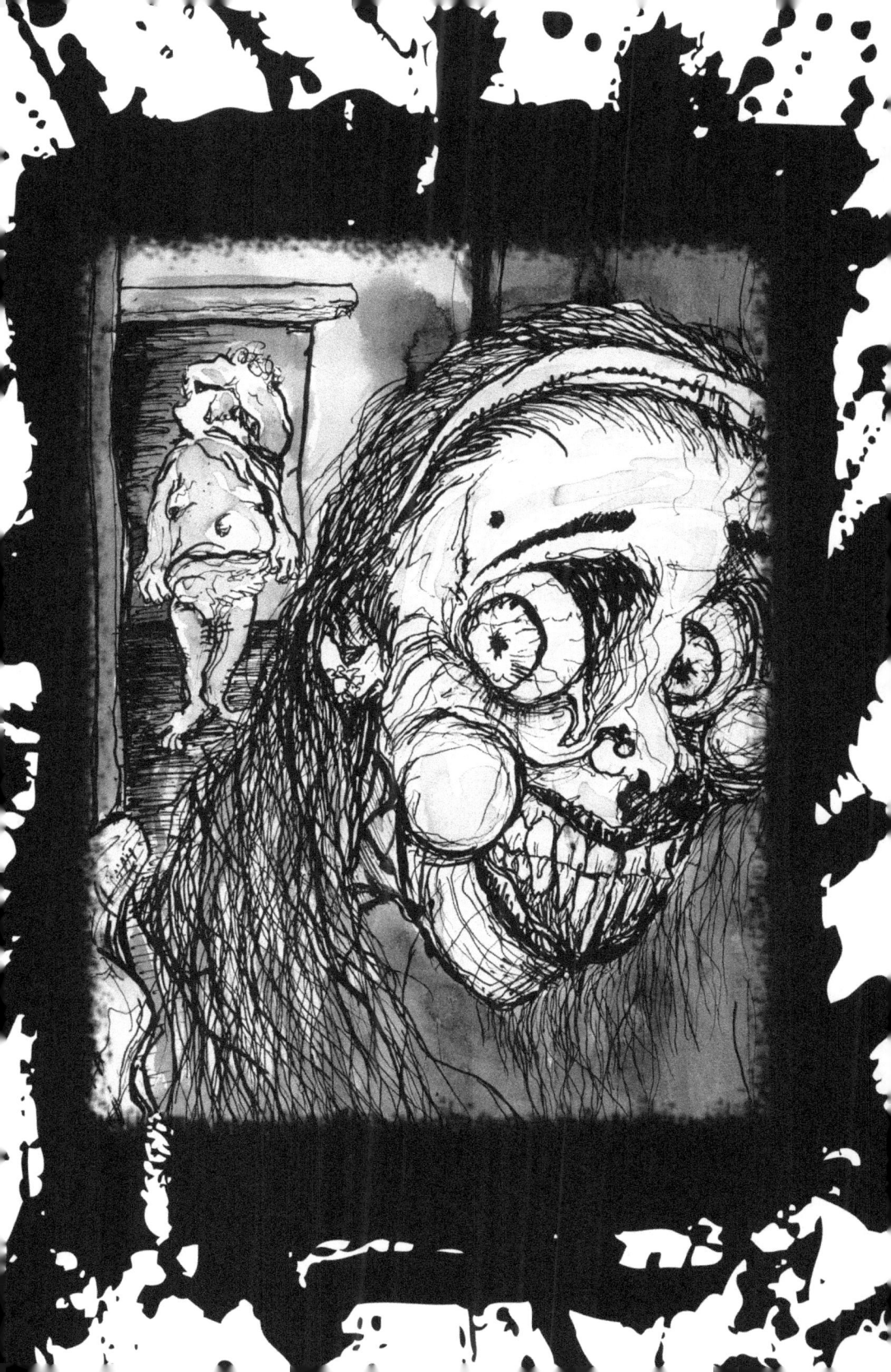

I couldn't concentrate

I couldn't concentrate

I couldn't

"PENIS PENIS PENIIIIIIIS"

The concerned face of a young woman

Waited for my response

I couldn't concentrate

"PENIIIIIIIIIIIIIIIIIIIS"

A deformed mushroom

Blinked at me from below

Eyelids squelching together like swamp moss

And screams never ceasing

From the deranged voice around the corner

"PEEEEEEENIS PENIS PENIS PENIIIIIIIIS"

I couldn't concentrate

Penetrated by the phallic outbursts

That seemed headless and without a body

I could not concentrate

As the voice physically faded

With my removal from the premises

It mentally lingered

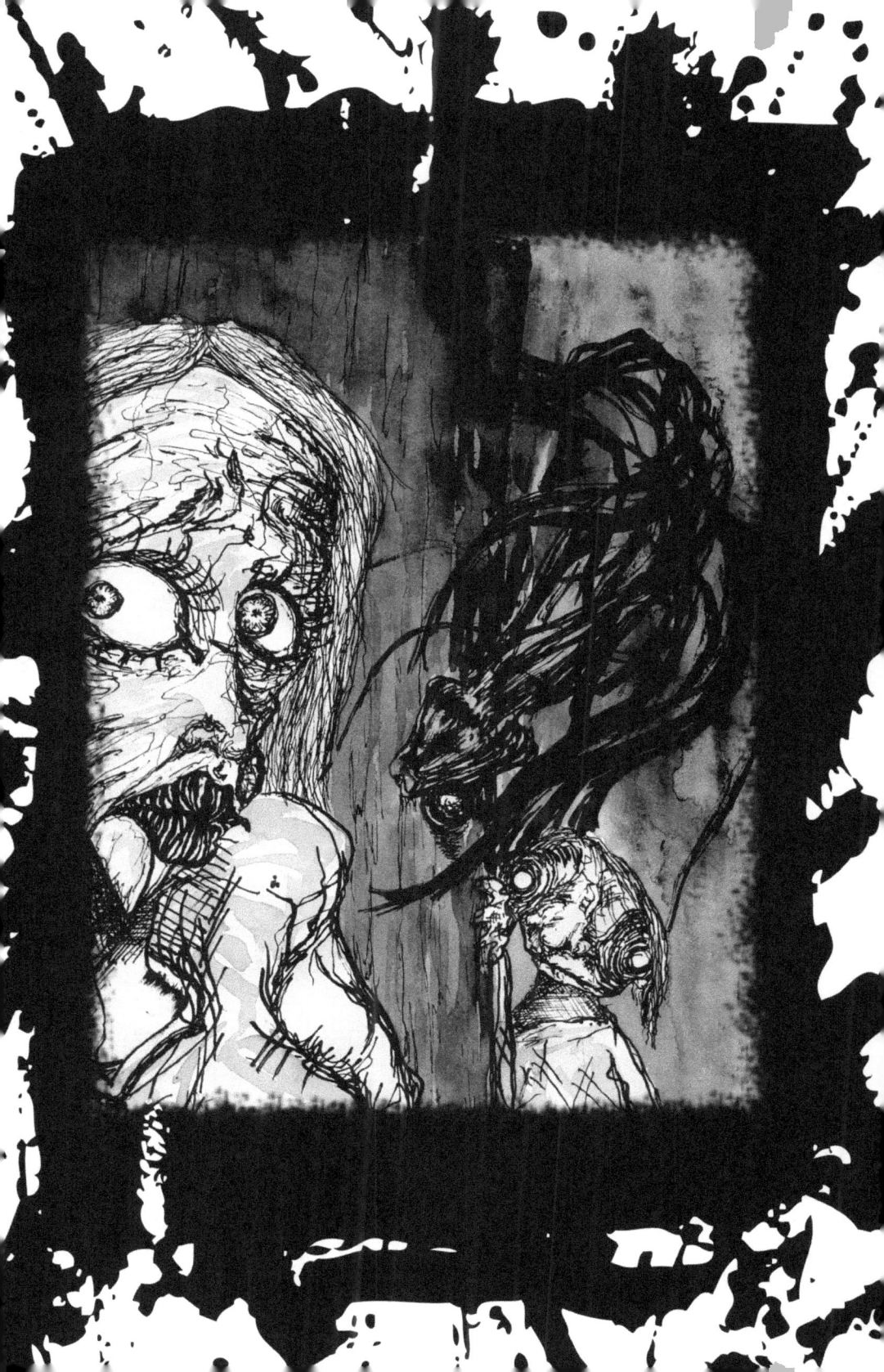

Each winding street roared

With the laughter of Midwestern birds

Sky the color of faded feathers

A sliding glass door

Like domestic lips

A woman glided to greet me

And an impish child pranced across the tile

Bare toes dancing through the carpet

Penis dangling like ruptured helicopter blade

Smile tickling the edges of his cheeks

As a feathery dollar thrust into my palm

And the lips pursed

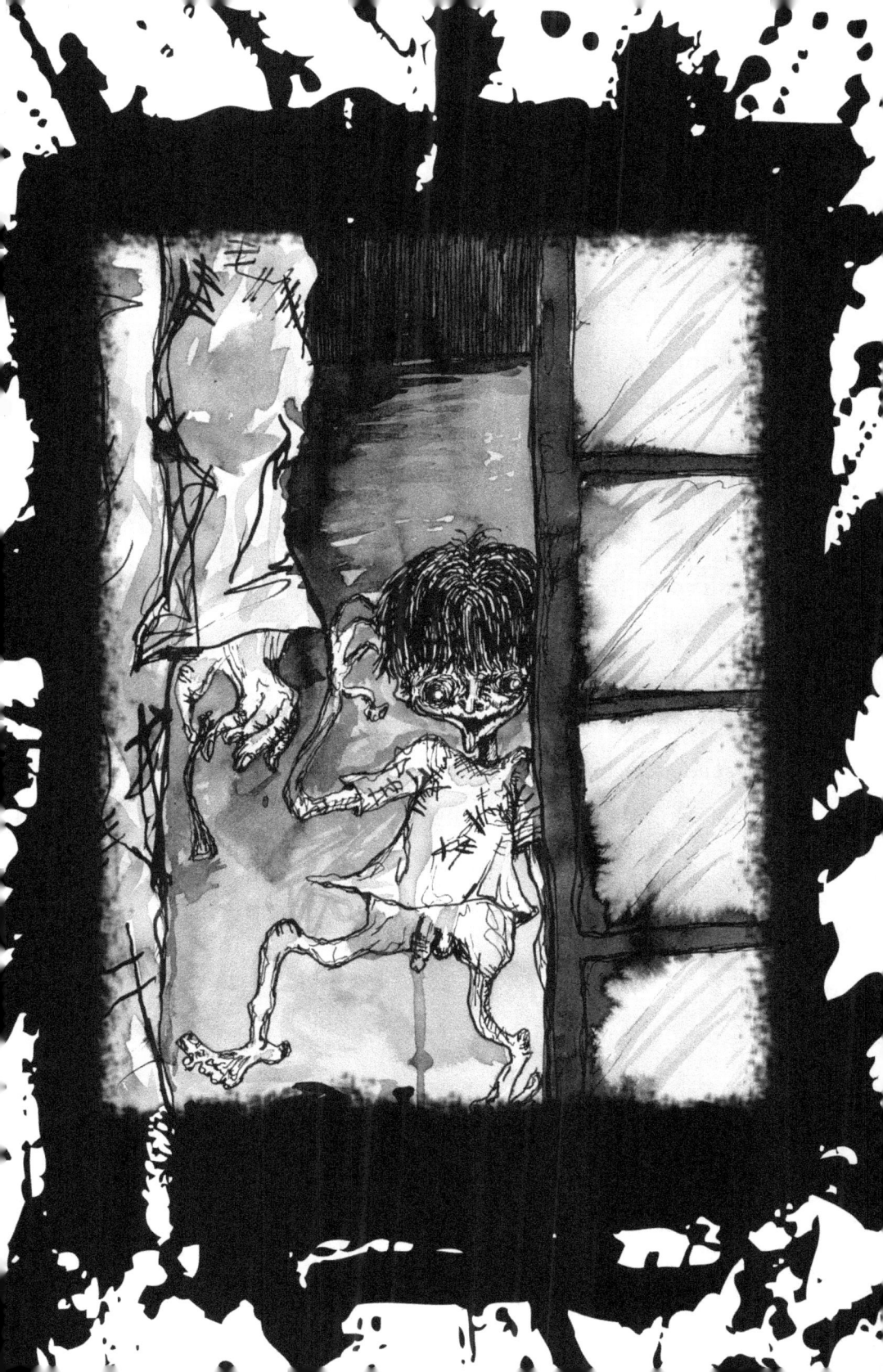

An explosion of child

A mess of baby teeth, small shirts and endless energy

This little shit threw himself on me

Arms ensnaring my legs

In an embrace?

There was relief in the child's voice

"Thank you Pizza Man"

My arrival seemed a steamy respite

To the child's greasy delight

Yet the spindly woman behind

Looked at me with fright

Or was it confusion?

I was the Pizza Man

Savior to this child

A story told at dinner

To dissuade the child

From any dreams that might cause him

To fly too close to the sun

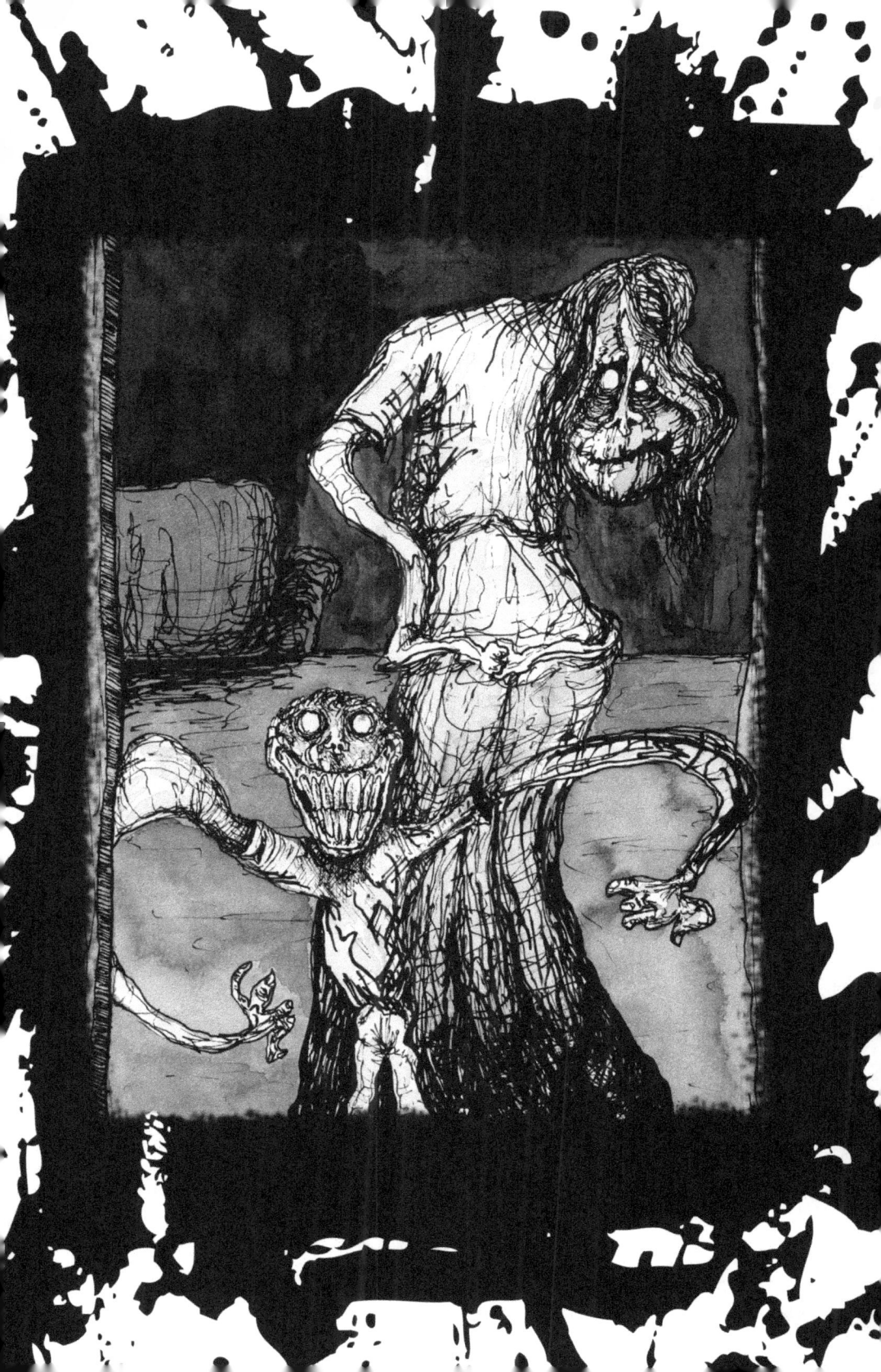

"Hold on, my uncle will just be a sec"

Wheezed a small child

Masked by the voice of a nicotine addict

The so called uncle steps into view

Built like an anorexic gorilla

His knuckles almost graze the linoleum

And mutters about pizza already paid

There is a small squeak above me

As the number zero hangs from its rusted nail

Threatening to break free

The low mumble of the uncle

Brings me back to reality

I hesitantly relinquish the pizza

Due to disoriented duty

Consequences pale in comparison

To the duo's shifty dealings

"Yeah, we gave them our credit card info three times"

As I walk away

I fear that their larcenous hands

Are already tearing away

At a pizza they had no right

To take

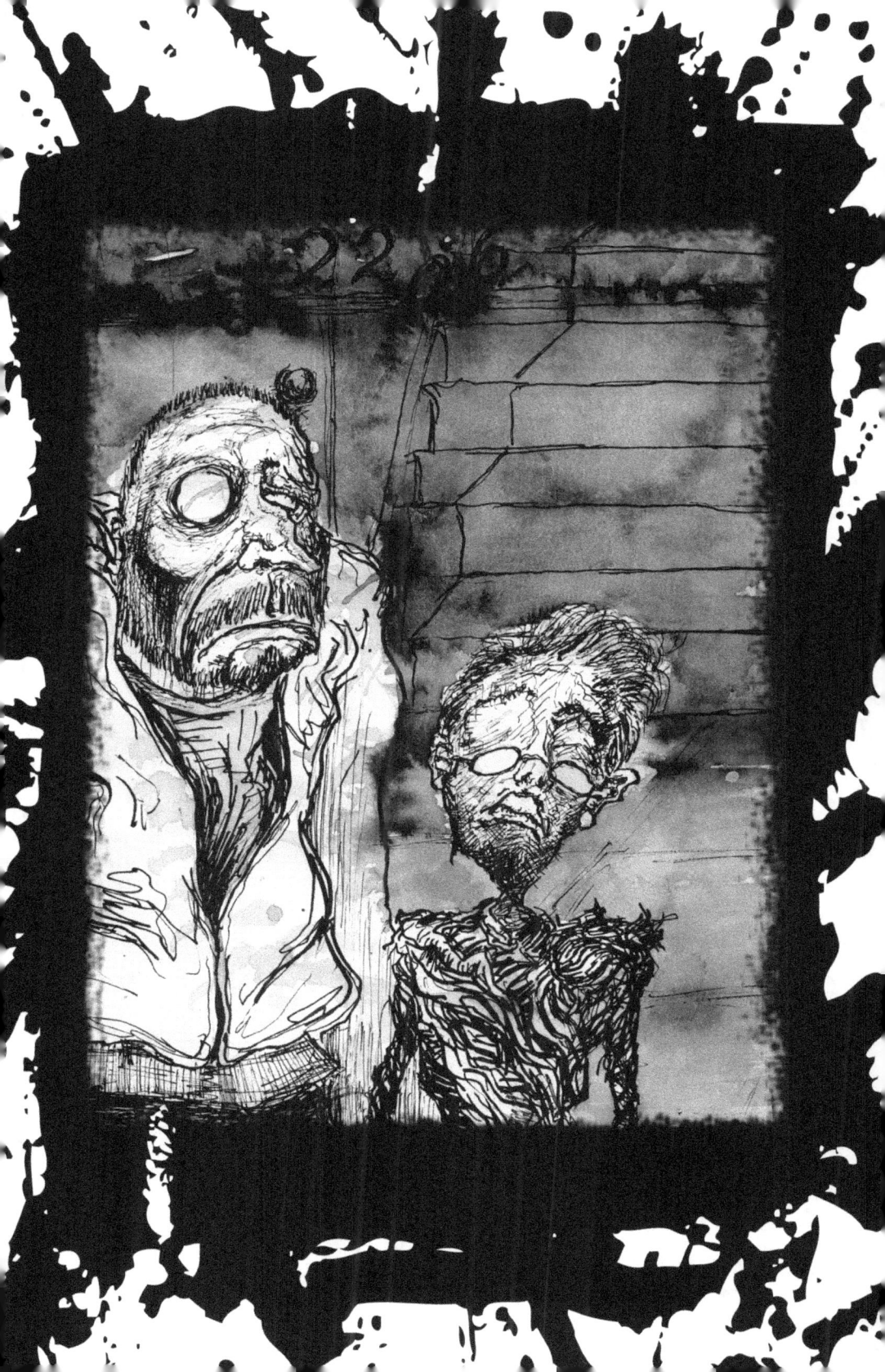

2205 Todd Drive

Where tips go to die

A man with hair like a Rick James

Cracked lips leaked

"I got this coupon for a free pizza"

And flashes a dimly lit image on his phone

But eyes registered nothing

As his face melted in drugged indifference

A brief phone call to Forrest

Awkward silence

A sluggish showdown

As I trudged away

Defeated

46

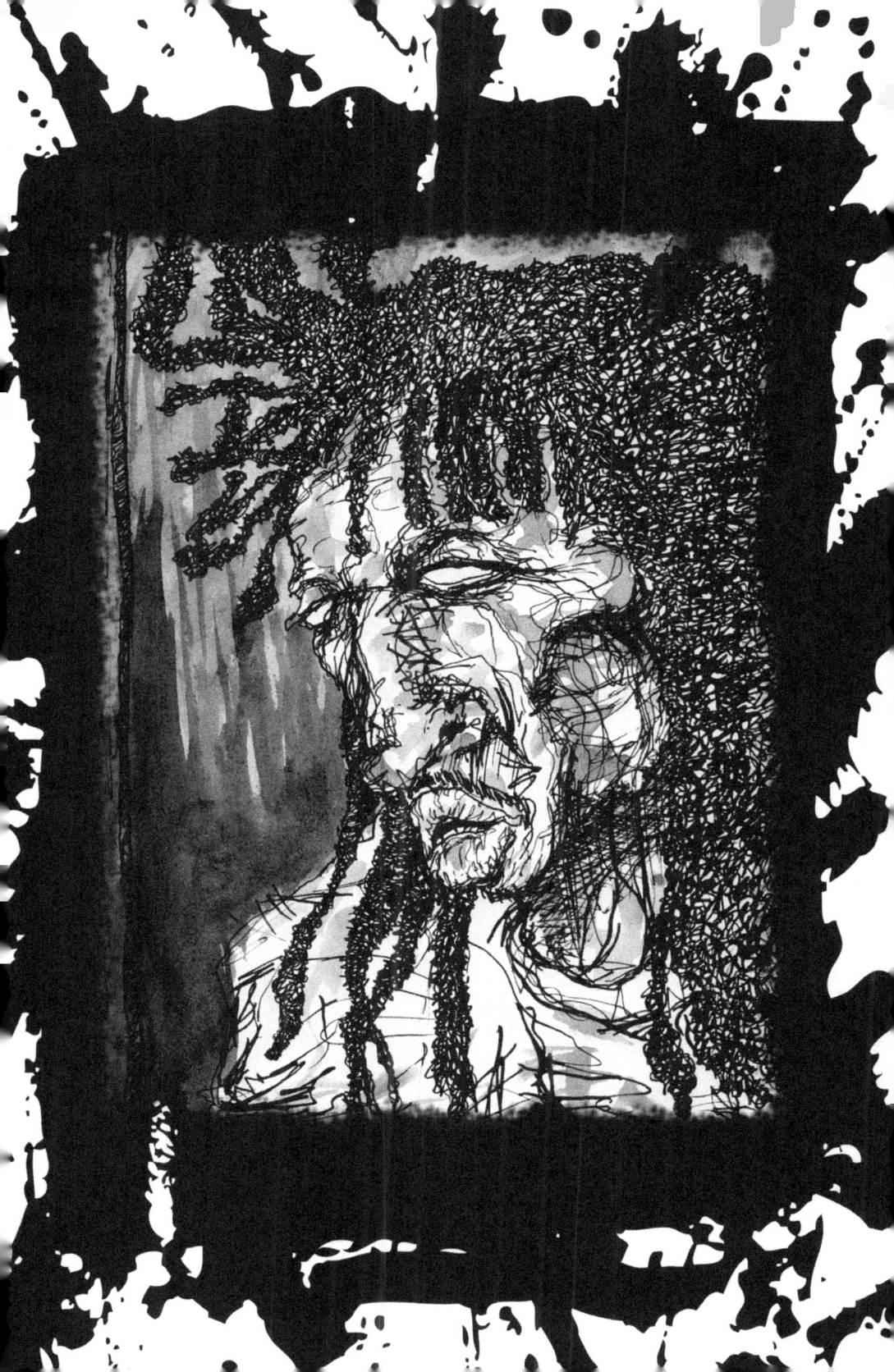

Purple shirt

Strangled the skin

Marked with the wrinkles of instability

Opaque octopus tentacles

Caressed the skull

The human hull

Heaving with impatience

Voice almost biting the air around us

But the dark eyes betray a weariness

Only amplified by the unhappy apartment

Walls sagging and fearing

The stranger at the door

The curt tone bleeds

With the sarcasm

As a vague veil

For depression

Nursed to death

By the dearth

Of high expression

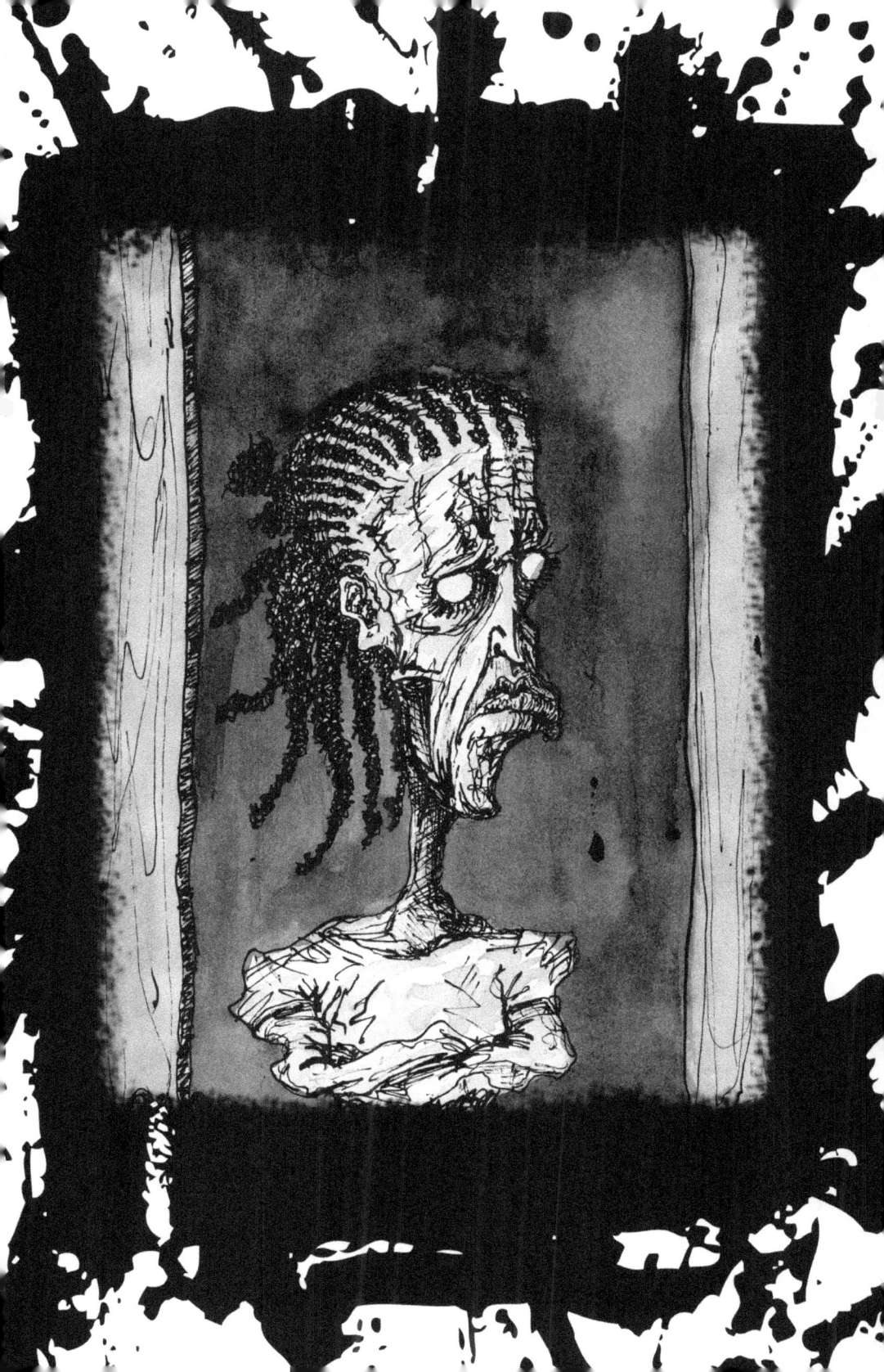

A clandestine apartment

Off the center of Currency Rd

Is suddenly wracked

By a roar

"DON'T ASK MY NAME"

A feral face grew from the edge of the door

An arm sprouted from that

Holding a phone

In the process of recording me

His eyes narrowed

Then spread like butter

Mouth flopping into hearty laughter

Savagery seemingly domesticated

By the steaming pizza

Veins breaching like whales

Came towards me

Gingerly accepting the pizza

Smile only threatening to widen

Metamorphosis

From paranoia to euphoria

Made complete

By the shutting of the door

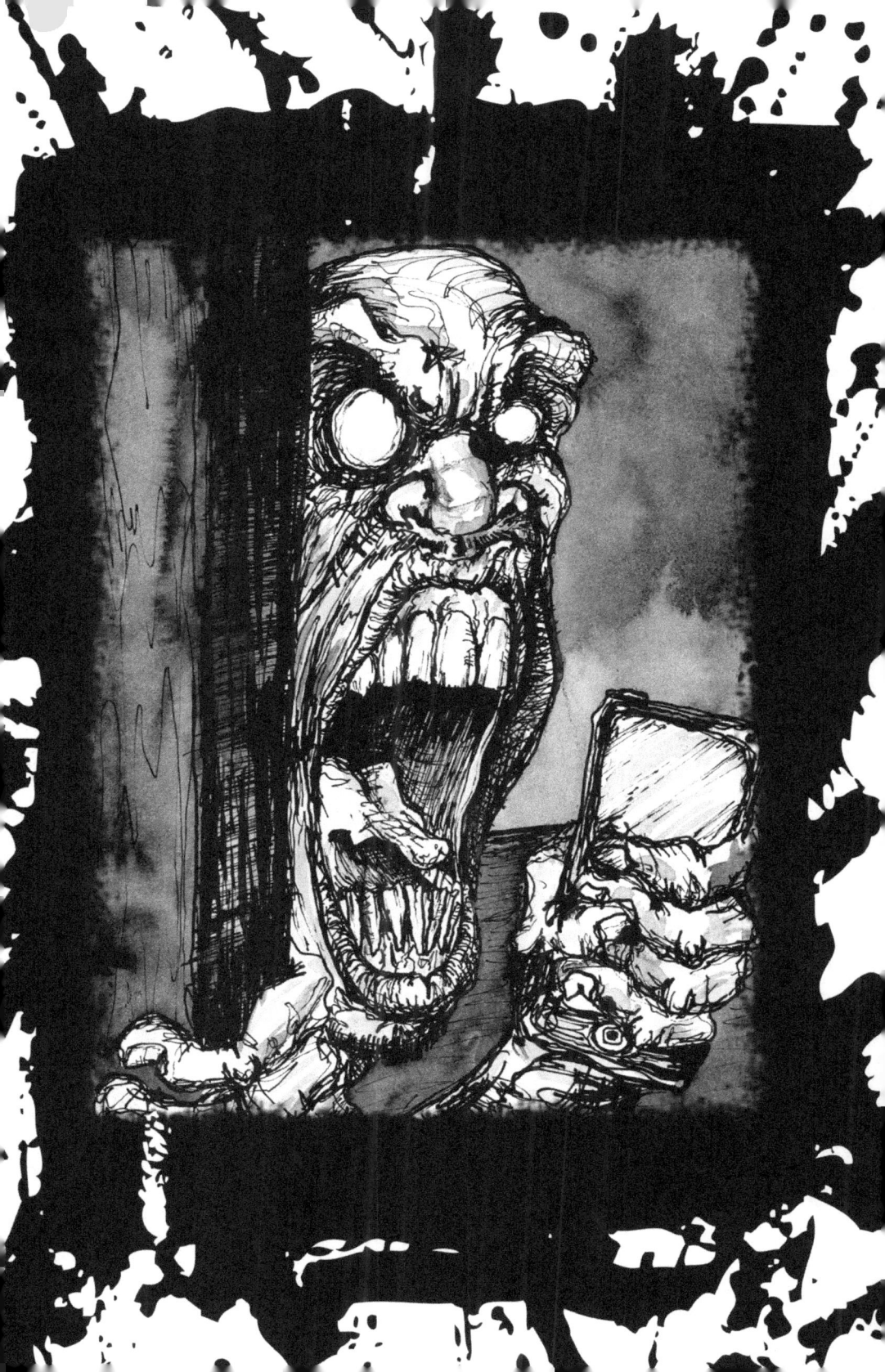

A gnarled Pinocchio

Stood as a husk of steroid and alcohol abuse

Muscles rippling, albeit nervously

With a face resembling a trashed scratching post

Gepetto must be long dead, I thought

This could only be the product of its master gone missing

Jagged and hunched over

As if the marionette strings still hung

Hanging just barely from his worn frame

His eyes seemed not to blink

As a wrinkled dollar presented itself

Indistinguishable from the crinkled skin of his fist

The dollar was an only child

"Don't worry, you'll get the rest later"

He wheezed, his eyes fixed motionlessly

The slow shutting of the door

Triggered a shiver

Which slithered up my spine

And I left with a quiver

Yet the sun continued to shine

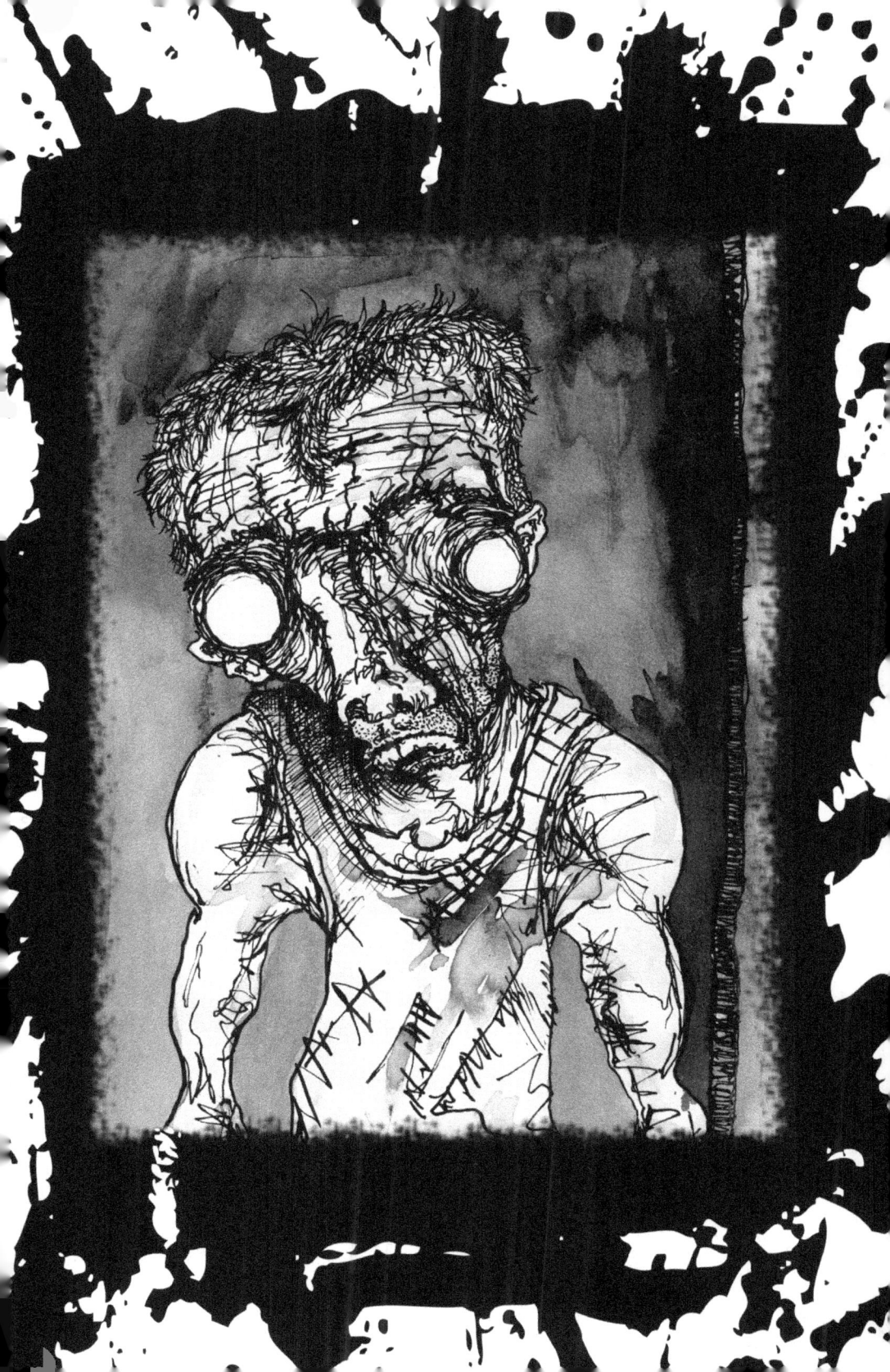

THIS DOOR IS LOCKED FOR YOURE PROTECTION

NOT MINE

Hesitant to knock

In fear that this sign

Might be true

A pinched squawk

Comes from behind the door

"Wait a minute, will ya?!"

A rotten plum of a man enters the light

With the care of a drunk

And the leer of a Republican

Bloodthirsty from the national convention

The exchange was short

And made without a further sound

Except for the obstinate slam of the grizzled door

Once again protecting me from whatever horror

I just ignored

Oh well, at least one more

Roy Rambo

His ancient face peered from the crack of the door

Each wrinkle like a deserted driveway

In the backwoods of the south

Voice like giant boulder

Slowly rolling down a dry mountain

His one exposed eye boiled me

In a pot of such intensity

That I began to hear planes flying overhead

Their engines barely masking

The distant sound of aerial explosives

Until fence like teeth splintered apart

"Thanks, man, I appreciate it"

I shook my head

Eyes rolling like pinballs

Boing

Bong

Bing

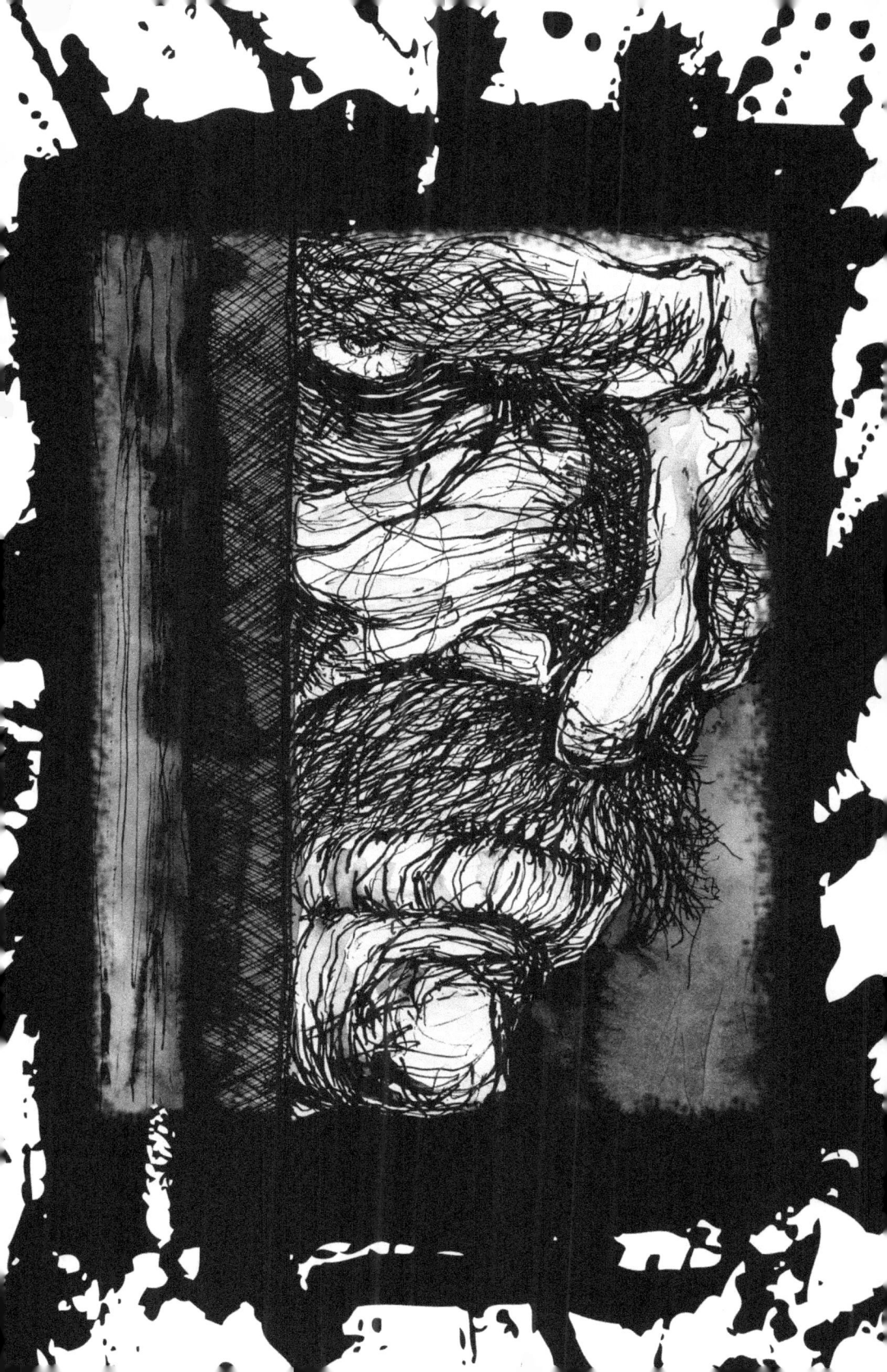

II. HOMES

The height of sedimentary complacency

Another drab suburban house

In a Levittonian array

Melting into the gray

Of the surrounding snow

The crinkle of my pocket

Betrays the woman's ruse

And the receipt whimpers

A feeble gratuity

Suddenly the door opens and the house exposed itself

A cheerful woman signs the waxy paper

The words "Live Generously" were
emblazoned on her shirt

A cruel joke or an oblivious mistake?

Stray thoughts blown free by the closing of the door

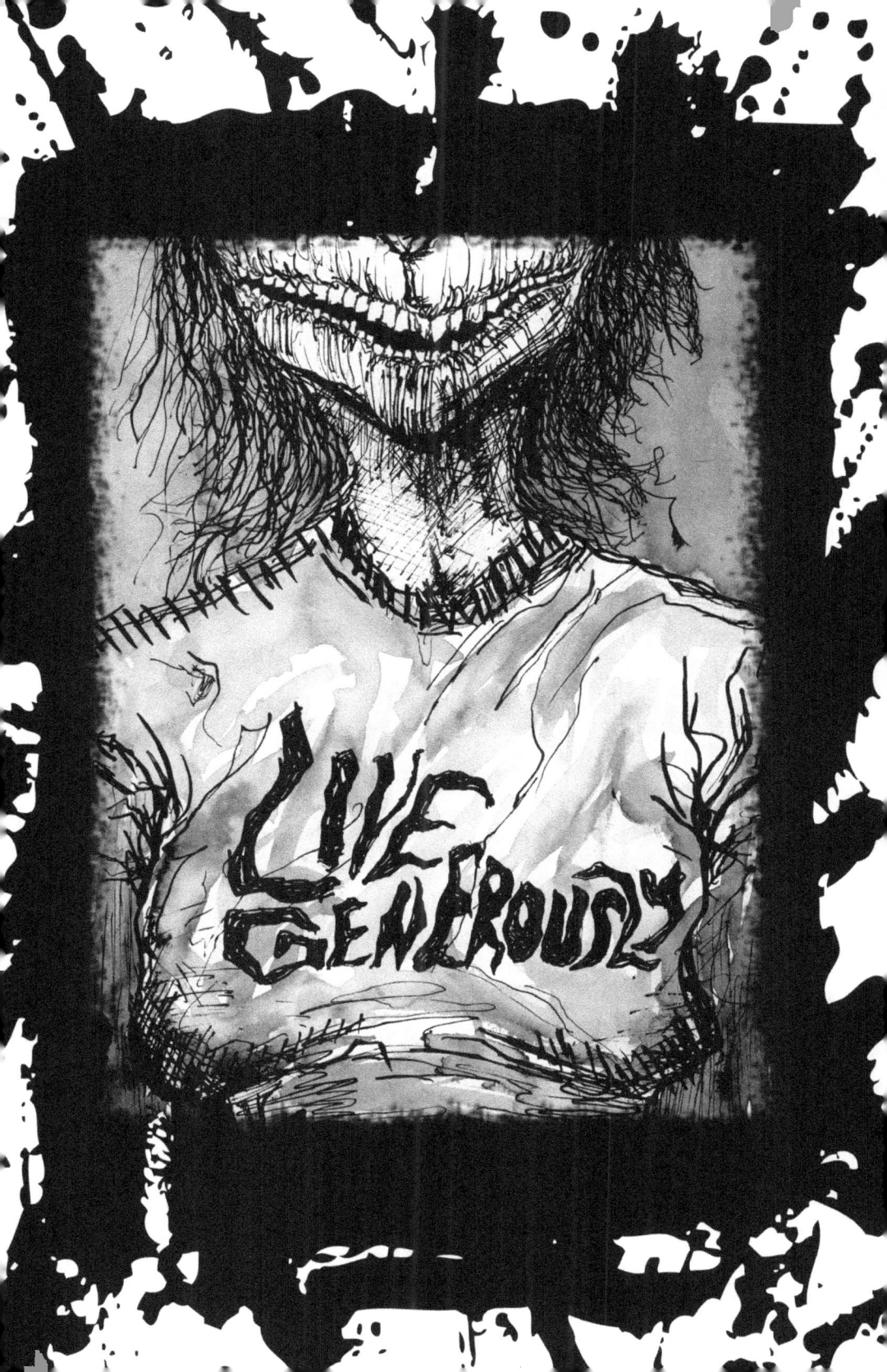

Gentledogs, start your engines!

Surely, it has started

The lolling tongue of the dog seemed to shout this

Only corroborated by the vibrations

Of his torso

Of the man I retained nothing

But upon my exit

Was immediately tracked down by the down

Halfway to the edge of the driveway

Cock splayed through the air

Sending an amber character liquid

On individual journeys of flight

Each coming to a bitter end

On the hairs of my legs

And their covering khakis

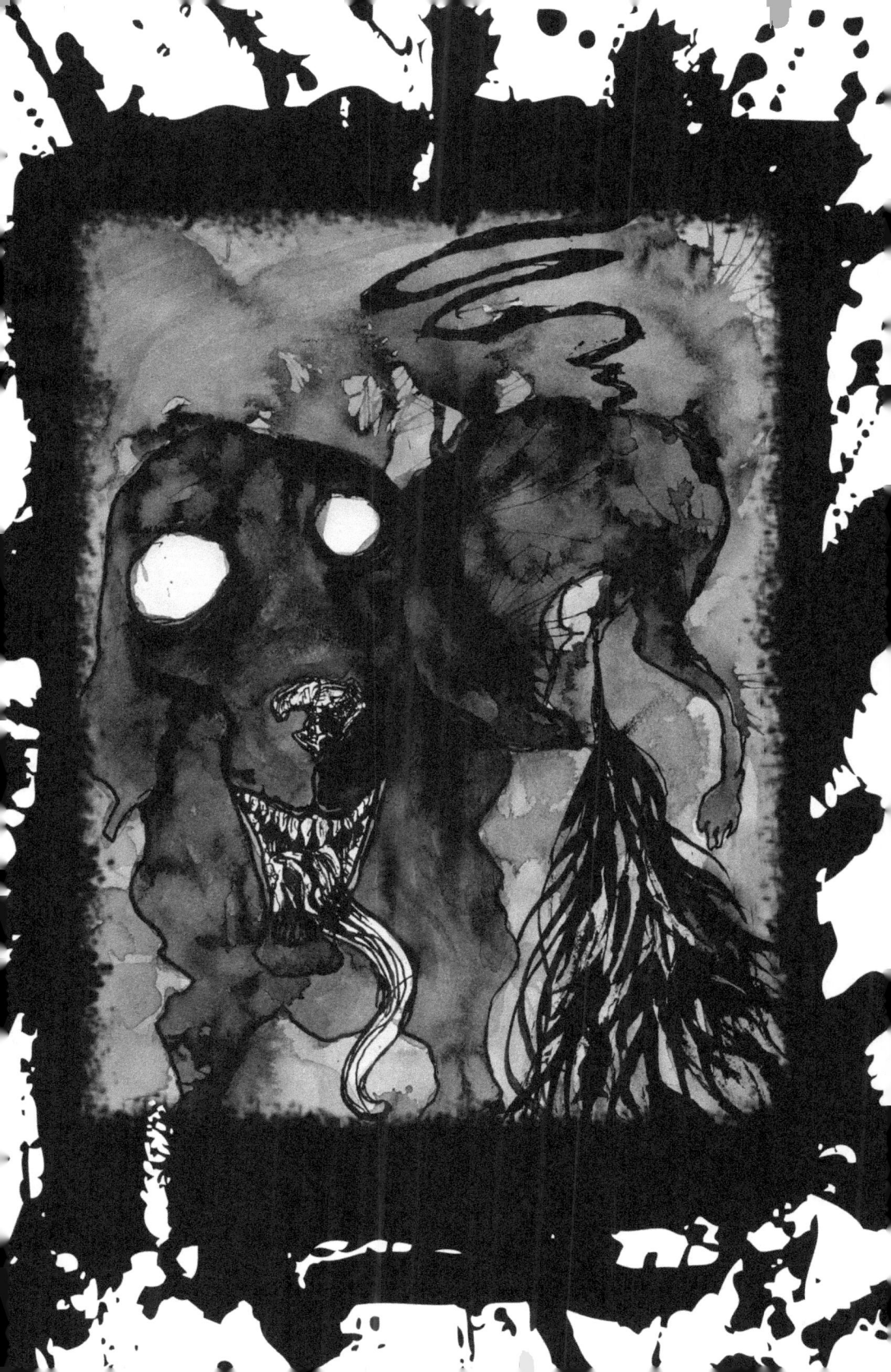

The skeletal branches

Shrouded the towering shade

Ballooning above me

Latex eyes staring down

With an implied frown

Almost folded arms

Swaying

As if reciting an incantation

Although threatening

Failed as a bodyguard

As I walked up to the door

Right past the obsolete eyesore

Our backs to each other

I greeted what was

A completely forgettable group of humans

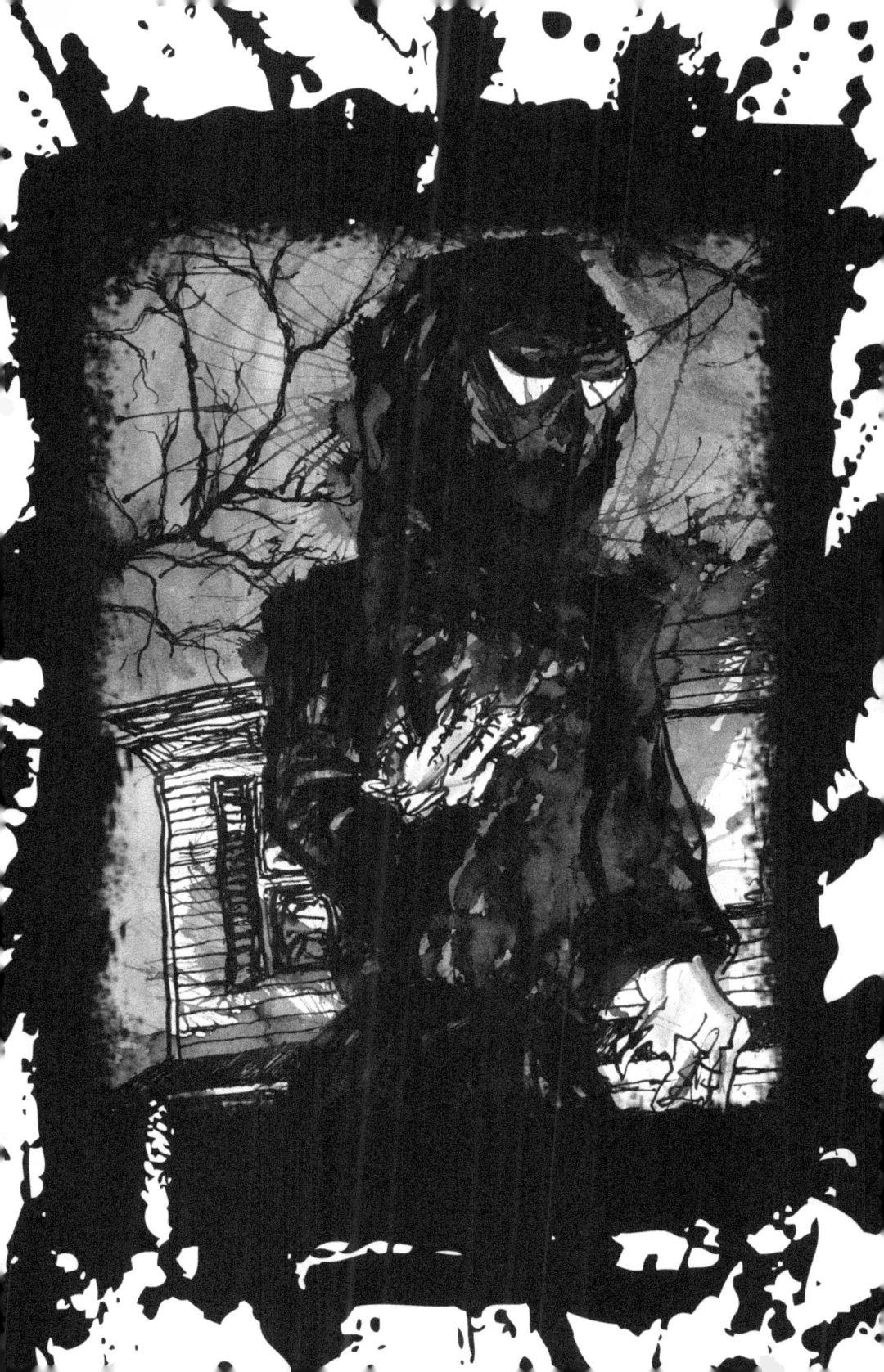

A hollow knock

On a cheap dollhouse door

And a plasticine figure walks into view

The Lady in the Radiator

Immediately a coldness cloaked me

Eyes excavated as dark pits extending for miles

As cracks ran down her face

Until forming a hard mechanical line

Where a mouth should be

Silence seemed to stretch indefinitely

Under her static gaze

Until the shutting of the door

Broke the trance and offered small solace

As I was returned to normal size

And the dollhouse became

A memory

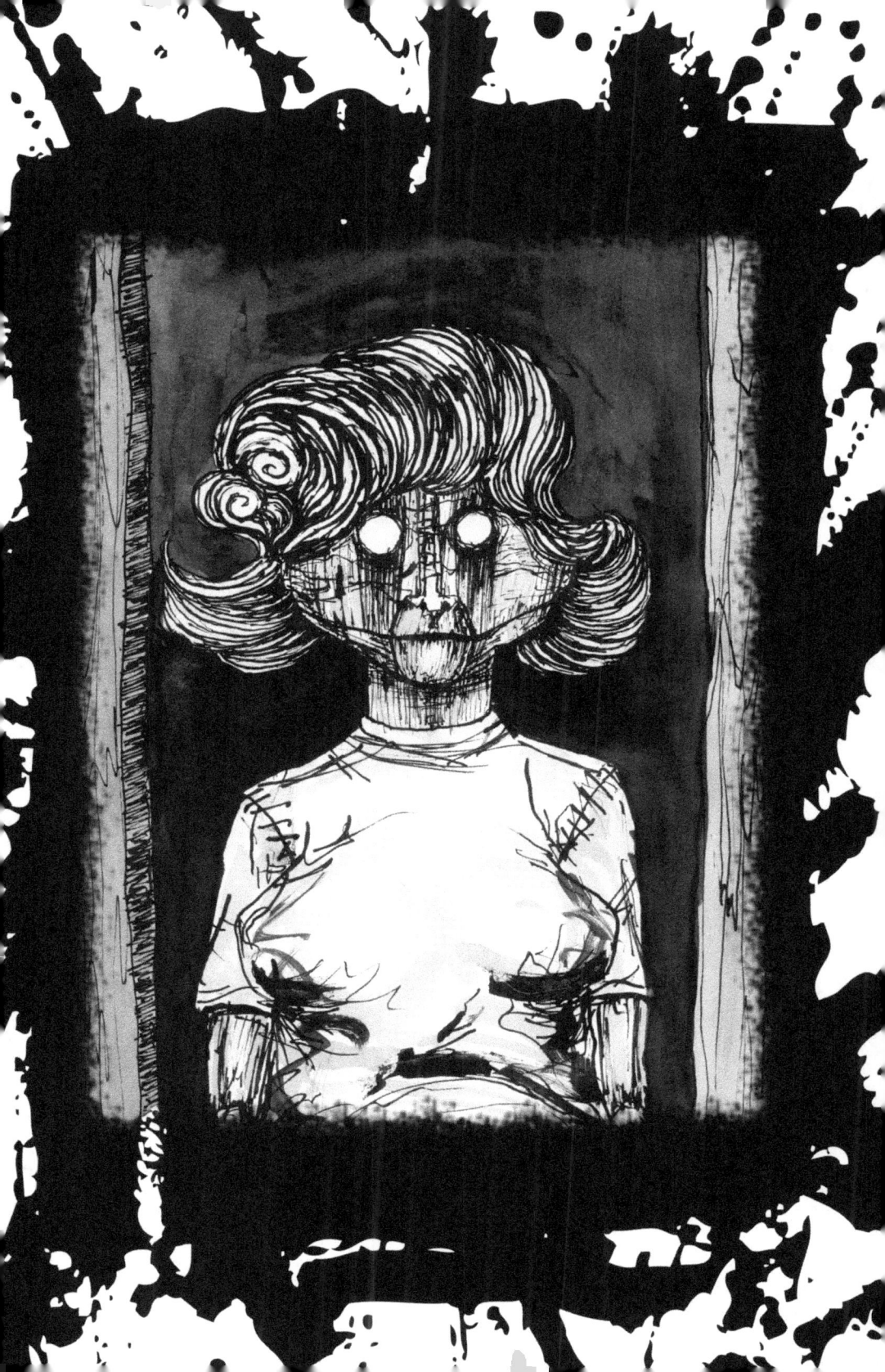

Average

Two high school girls

Standard levels of excitement

Until

Garage door

SLAM

The sound startling a swallow in a nearby bush

The image of a shriveled alien

With unidentified flying eyes

In powder blue pajamas

Bespectacled with childishly drawn flowers

Framed by a doorway of red brick

As I passed off the pizza

A shadowed gremlin grabbed its arm

"Oh shit"

And dragged her slowly into the shadow

The door tip toeing shut

A hard contrast from its opening

Just about as hard as those bricks

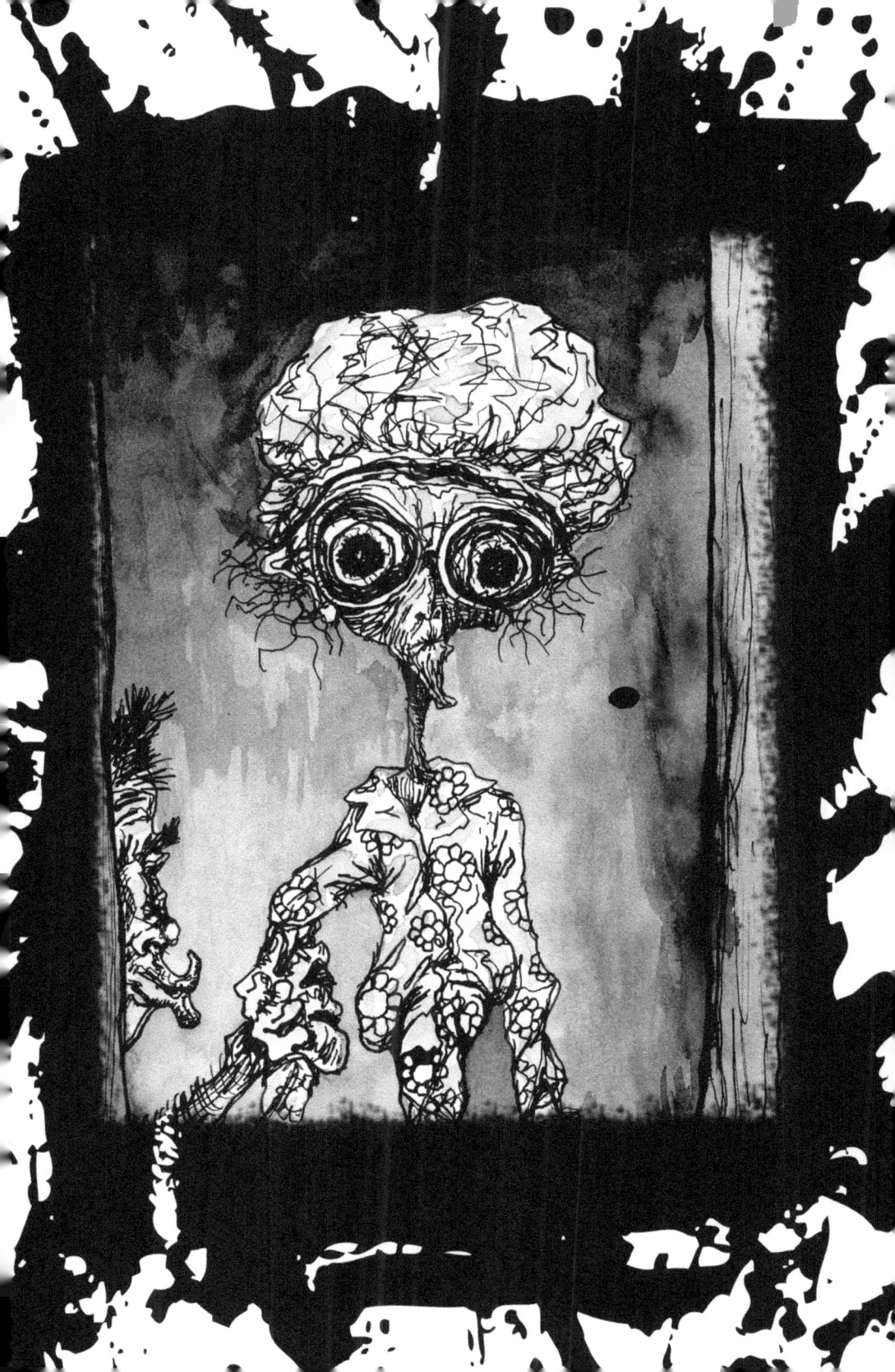

The whirring of an eight wheeler split in two

Stops simultaneously

As a similarly clothed man walks out

Black and red with Jimmy John's

On the same path

Shoes step in synchronicity

Until we are shoulder's length

Like Siamese twins

Exchanging furtive glances

As we silently decided

Whose clenched fist

Would collide with the false mahogany

A woman shaped like a novelty gourd came out

Arms spreading and connecting at the hip

"Well isn't this funny?!"

We looked at each other

As we handed her a pizza and a sandwich

And began our mitosis

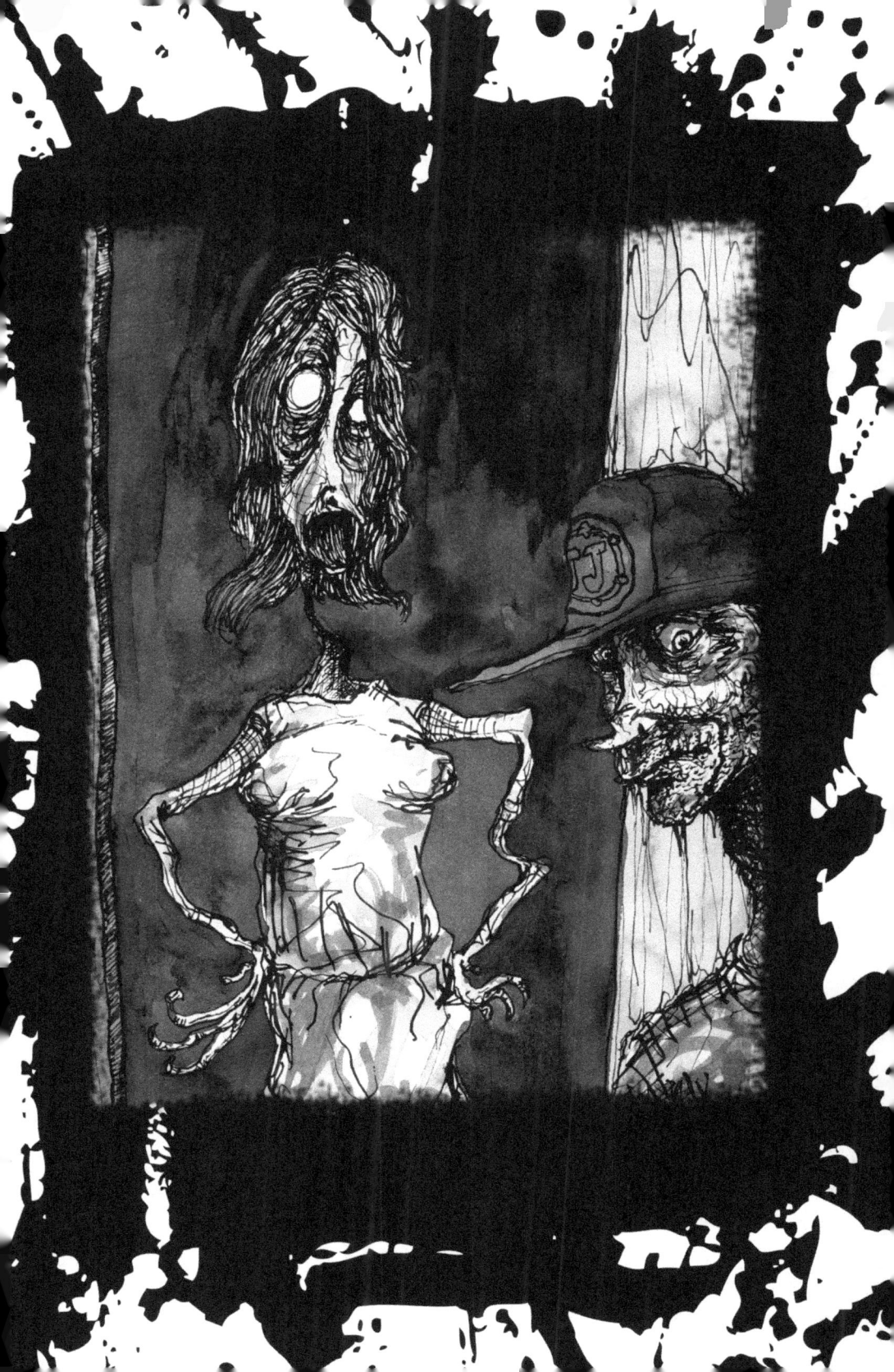

The Iowa Hawkeyes

Glaring at me from both breasts

Of both bug eyed smiles

Teeth seemingly treacled shut

By an eerie enthusiasm

Reminiscent of the socially despondent qualities of androids

Just jettisoned from the factory

No one is this single minded

Are they?

Their words vibrate

Like the pre-programmed phrases

Heard by the pull of a drawstring

Of a talking doll

Smiles never ceasing

As they stood, decreasing

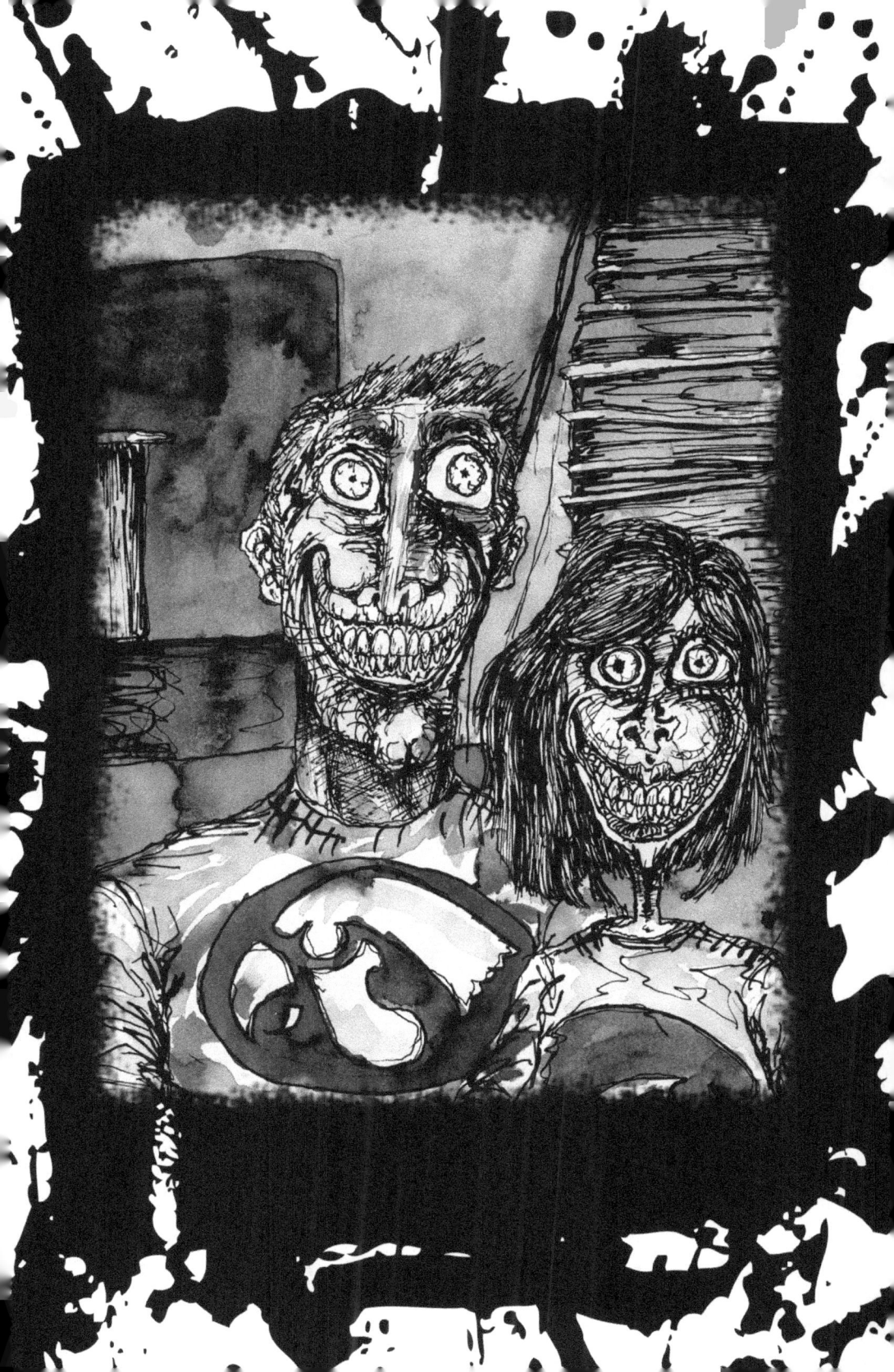

Waiting

Two eyes lock with eight

And forms a kinship

Friends of fur and flesh

Living since halcyon days

Disturbed by the swinging of varnished wood

Eight more eyes meet mine

Swelling of youth

With voices like songbirds under the foot

And a matriarchal presence sqwawks

A shrill scream collides with the peaceful
arachnid

Chased down by a ruby red adorned palm

celebrated unceremoniously by a thud

And a glazed grin grows as wide as the door

At the sight of the obsidian smear

And the friendship

From before

Remains a thankless fear

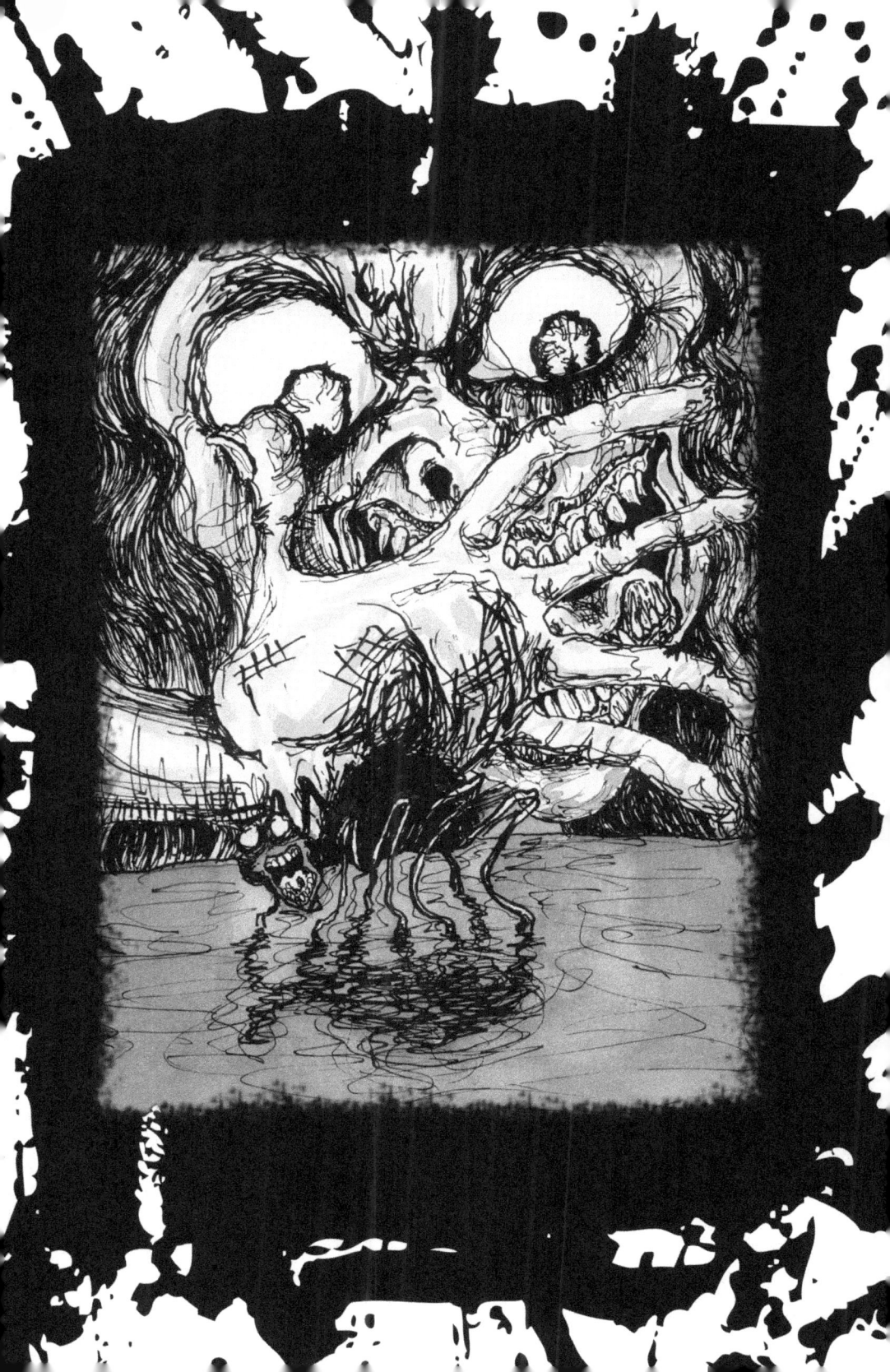

The doorbell snickered as the suburban tranquility

Was massacred by an overzealous television

Two flickering figures appeared in brief illumination

Lit only by the blue light of Deadpool

Soundtracked by explosions and sarcasm

Suddenly sucked dry of any sense of hearing

COULD YOU TURN THIS SHIT DOWN?

My mind screamed

But I guess I didn't hear it

Or couldn't hear it

Mouths flapped noiselessly and hands trembled

Assembled by instinct

As flashing fingers scrawled

The recognizably illegible signature

In the pink ink of a bloated pen

Raucous explosions

Expelled me from the indoor calamity

Back into the typical tranquility

Of the dark street

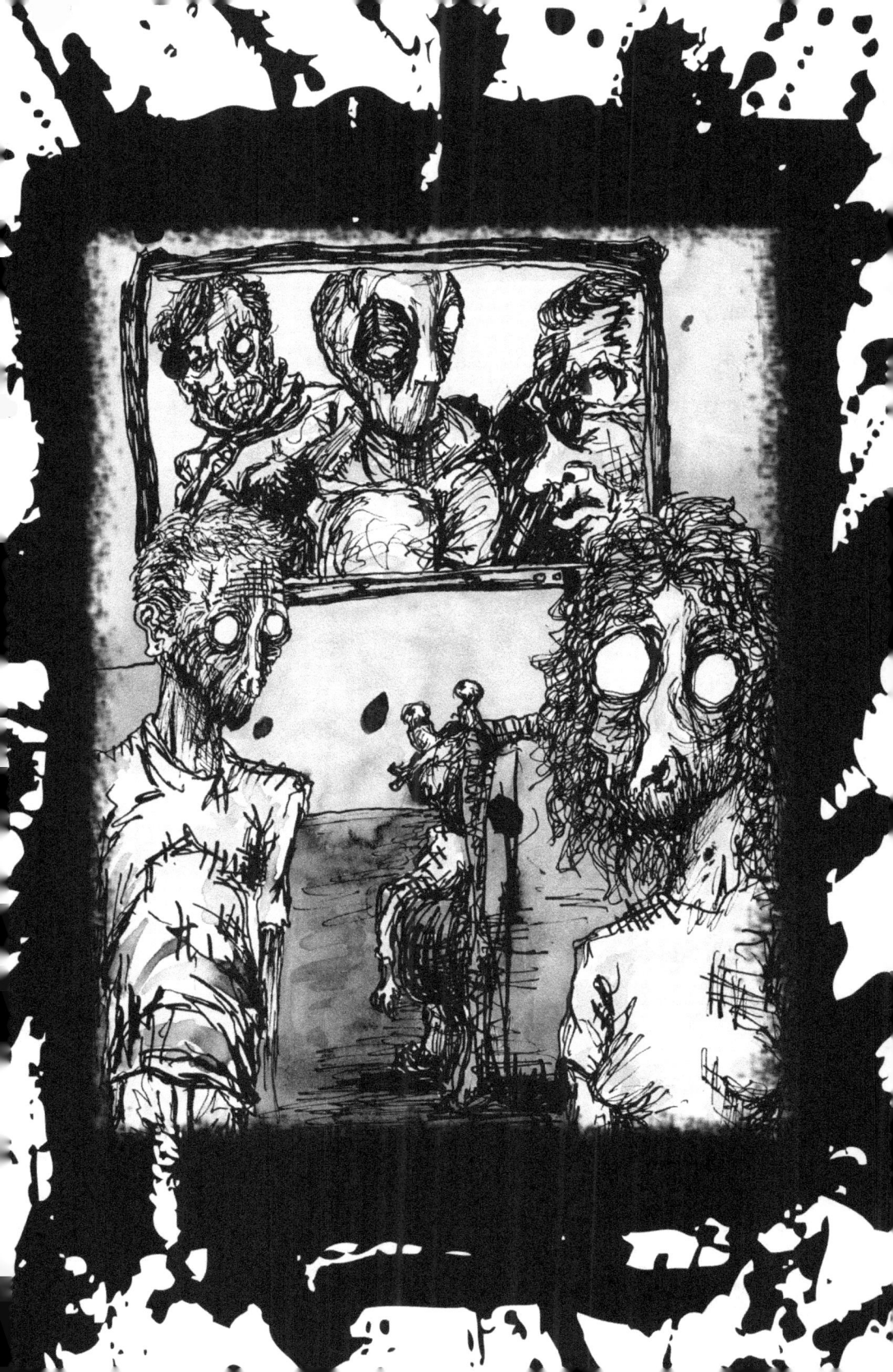

SEND ERIC NOVAK

The receipt howled back at me

With a familiar name stamped in wax

"Is that your shorty?"

Quipped Forrest at the register

If he only knew her

His sentence would crumble under the weight

Of its own ludicrousness

A short distance

To Sennett Studios

The silence of the night

Sliced by Kate's sarcastic snarl

And Cale's cool drawl

For moments

The job melted away

Held hanging in the night

By bonds of friendship

A reminder of the world

Outside the oiled grasp of John Schnatter

As the darkness gradually changed to light

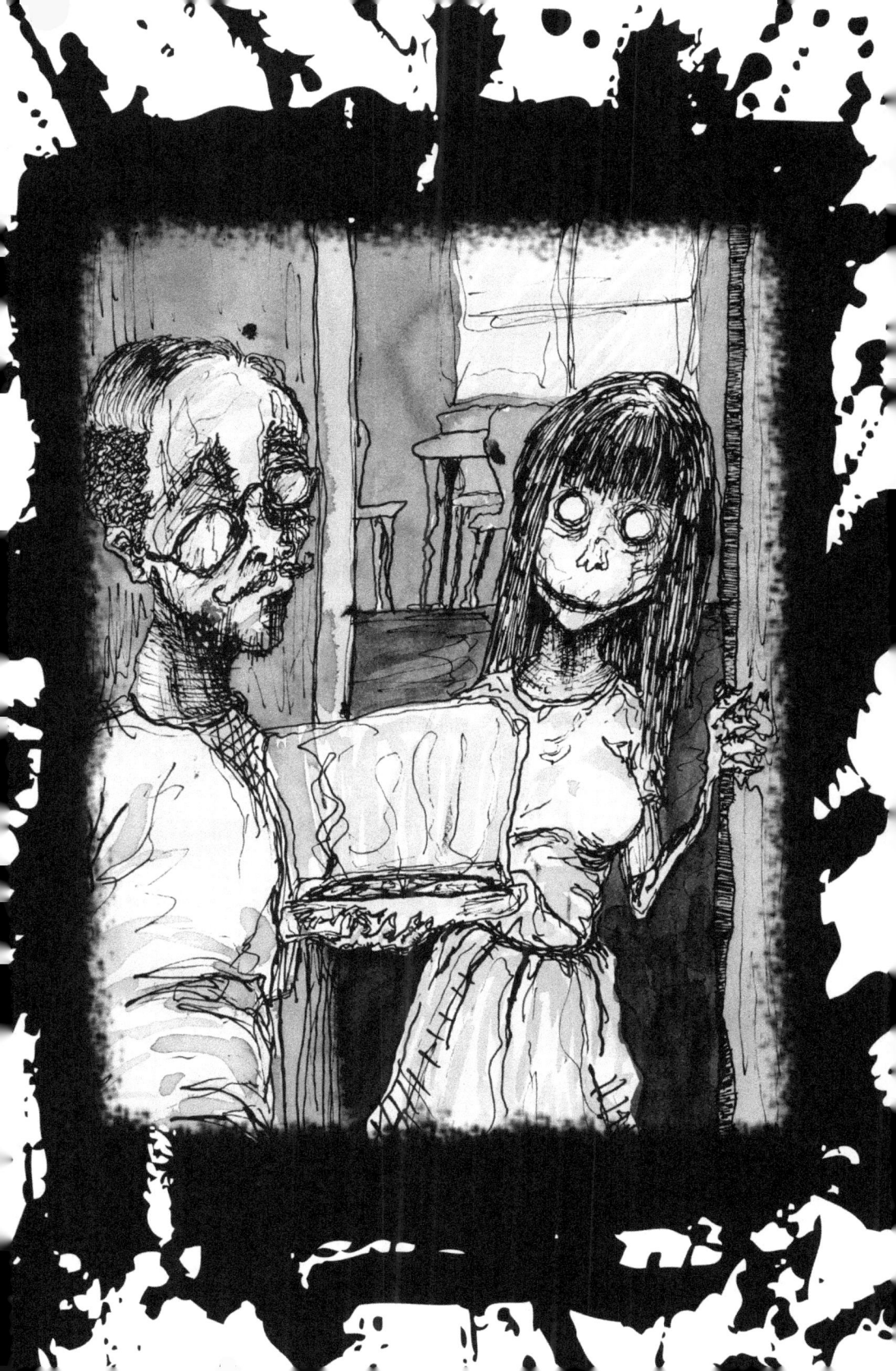

Emerson Street

A street I knew well

Held together by neglect

The house was small

But two beefy humans emerged

Their lips spun into a spoiled snarl

Their eyes focused on whatever was behind me

Barely registering my appearance on their step

The man had a facial junkyard

Of star shaped steel and coiled wire

Faded paint on his rusted cheeks

The woman was a rotund affair

Living in a personal orbit

Hair long and matted

By secretions of some animalistic order

They had a vague humanity

As if evolution forgot to finish the job

Somehow integrated and functioning

In such a low risk town

Emitting only grunts

They took the pizza

And retreated

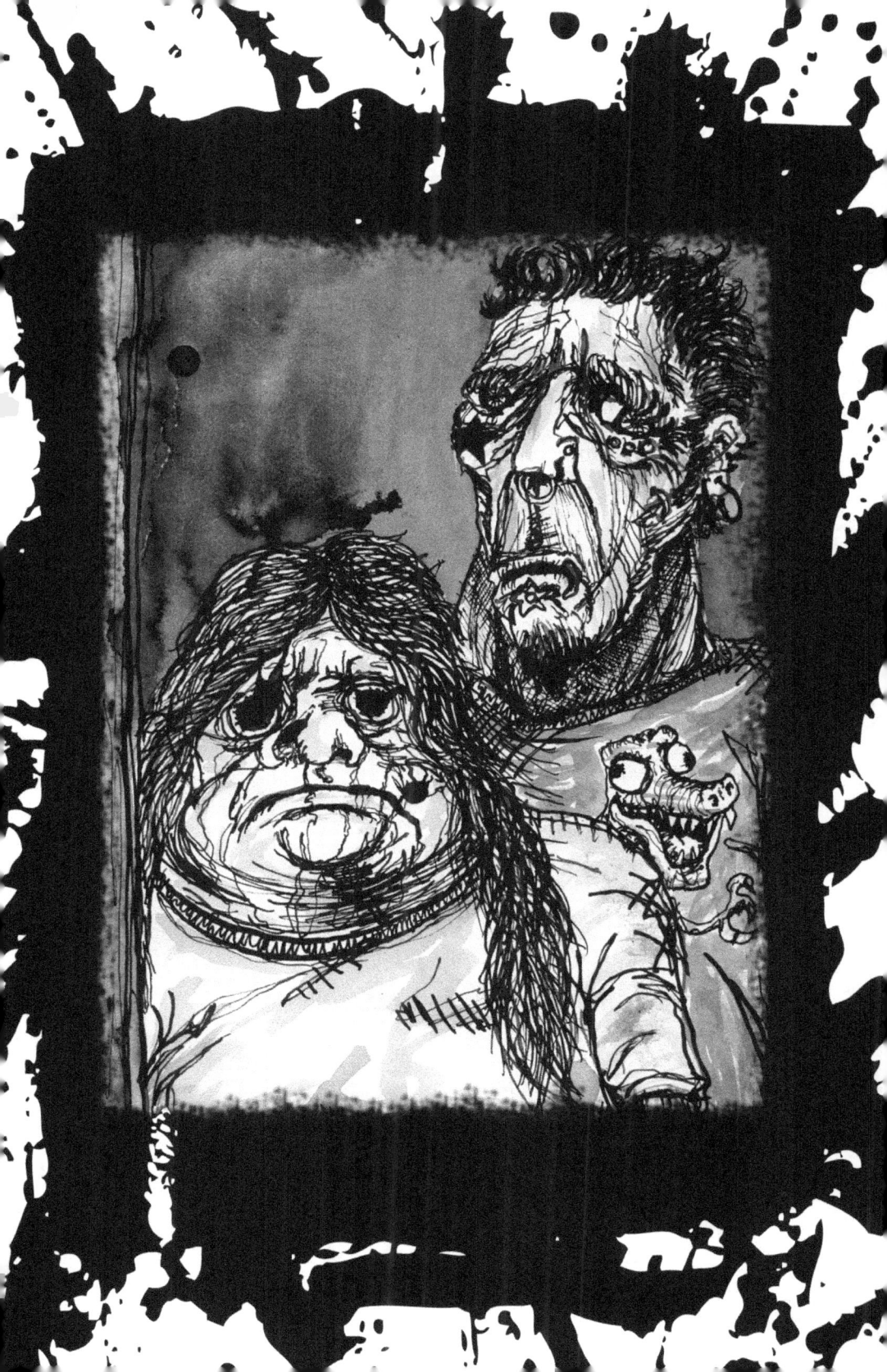

The receipt

A commonly conniving bastard

In a last ditch effort

Sent me reeling into a farce

Remedied by cellular redirection

And a bearded man with the nose of a bull

Peered at me through wired tunnels

As it began to rain

Rain droplets beginning to reflect

Blood and sapphire hues

White wails bouncing between the drops

From all directions

Circling the block

Rain drops growing more agitated

In an effort to drown out the sirens

Compete for my aural attention

As the bearded wall of indifference

Turned like a possessed chess piece

And left me to disappear behind

The patriotic plume of rain and sound

Forming over my head

No sign of Hercules

Or Darth Vader

This man was my dime store James Earl Jones

No fierce summer friends

No big pickle

Just a pizza

And a portly tub of lard

With a collection of now useless baseball artifacts

His shirt just continued the intellectual beating

Of his single minded hobby

He didn't even bother to search outside

The red down of fan loyalty

"I'm related to the man responsible for the billy
goat curse"

Seemed to trigger rusted furnaces in his eyes

Inviting me into his nostalgia encrusted cave

Voice booming with the energy of a man long gone

The voice of a man once stripped of a son

Long before he could even pick up a baseball

And left with none

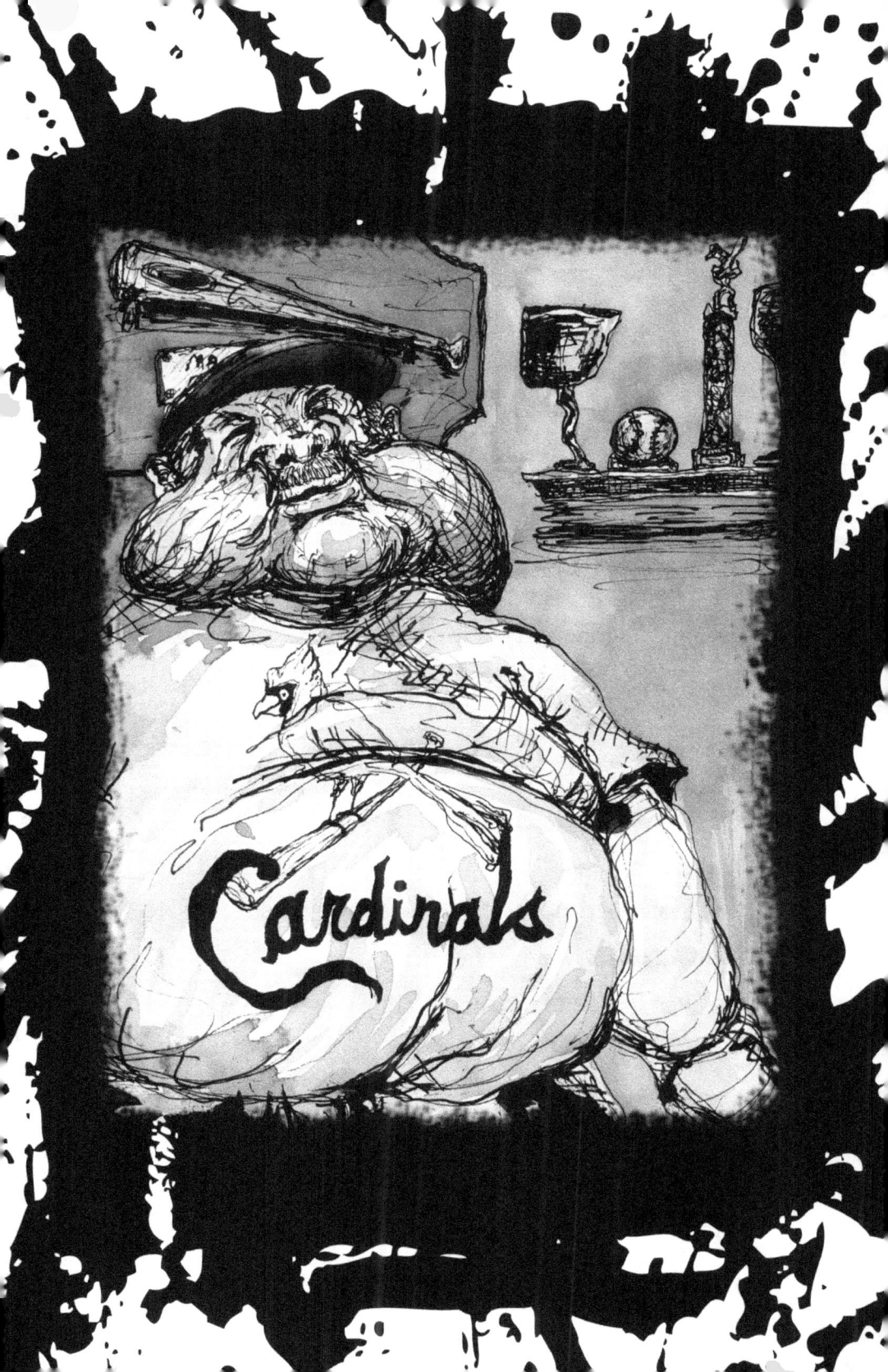

The door inched open

With the careful dedication

Of an ant carrying a pebble

And an overwhelmingly gray stick of a man

Frowned deeply

Hair like a jungle thicket

After a confrontation with a machete

Threatened to leap from his scalp

His face was a creased brochure of regret

Chin peppered with mistaken flakes of spilled seasoning

Cracking open to form the words

"I have not had a good day today"

As if this information was essential

For the success of the delivery

Monochromatic briefs

To mask any stains

Hung loosely from wires of his hip

Casting a shadow

On his awkward feet

Splayed about like a flattened bug

And he melted back into the surrounding gray

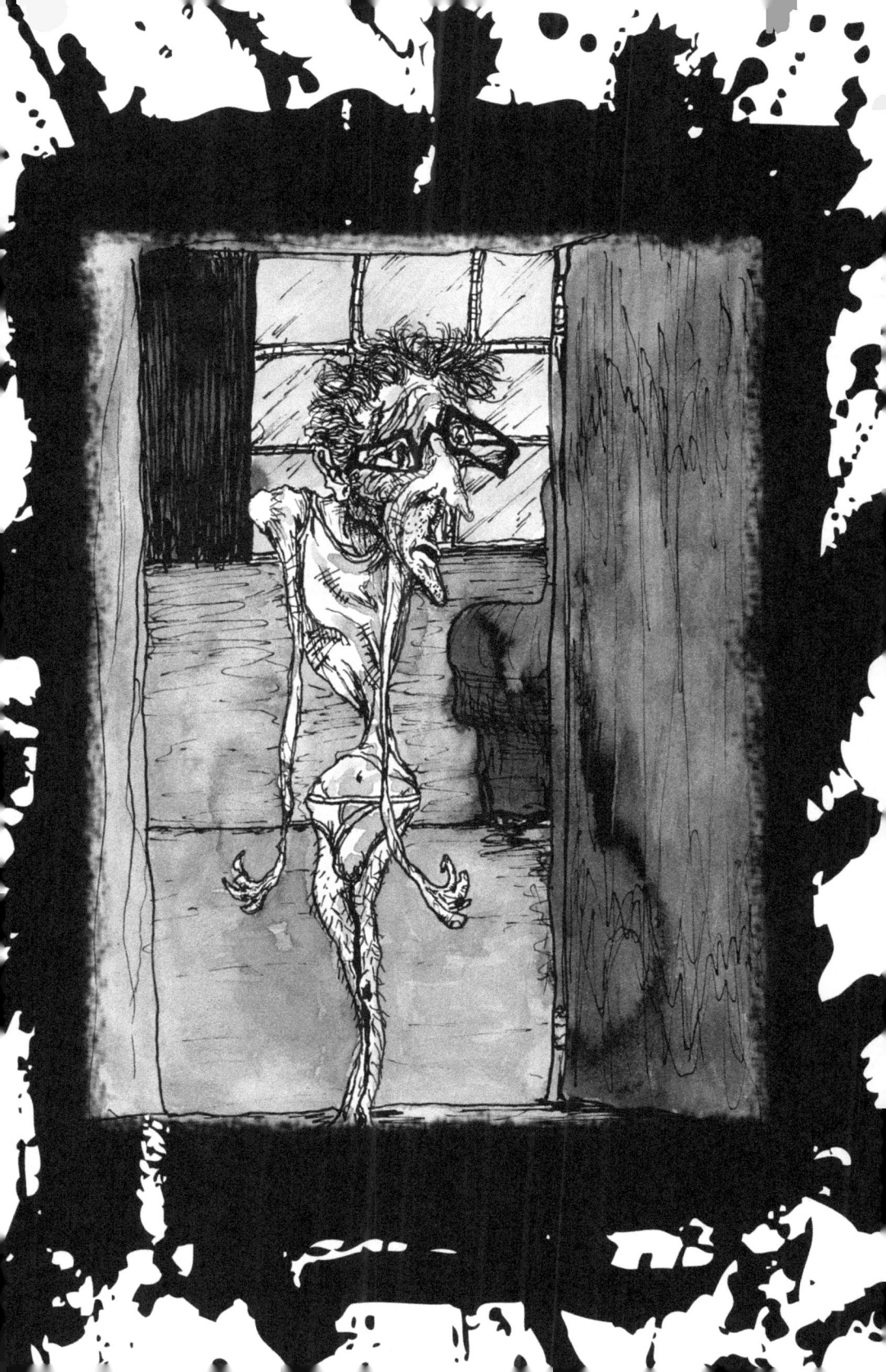

A warning sputtered from the salmon phone

While the gravel churned beneath

The tired treads of a dying jalopy

It was Kirsten

"She ain't happy"

I knew my pocket would starve

Just as steam wafted menacingly,

Swerving patiently

Until the screeching stop sent them

Intertwining with nature's fabric of scents

At the door

Opened casually

The risk of fatality

And a woman snatched from me

That which was already hers

Without so much as a transfer of words

The pizza bag lay defeated on the cement

Its lament of a life quickly spent

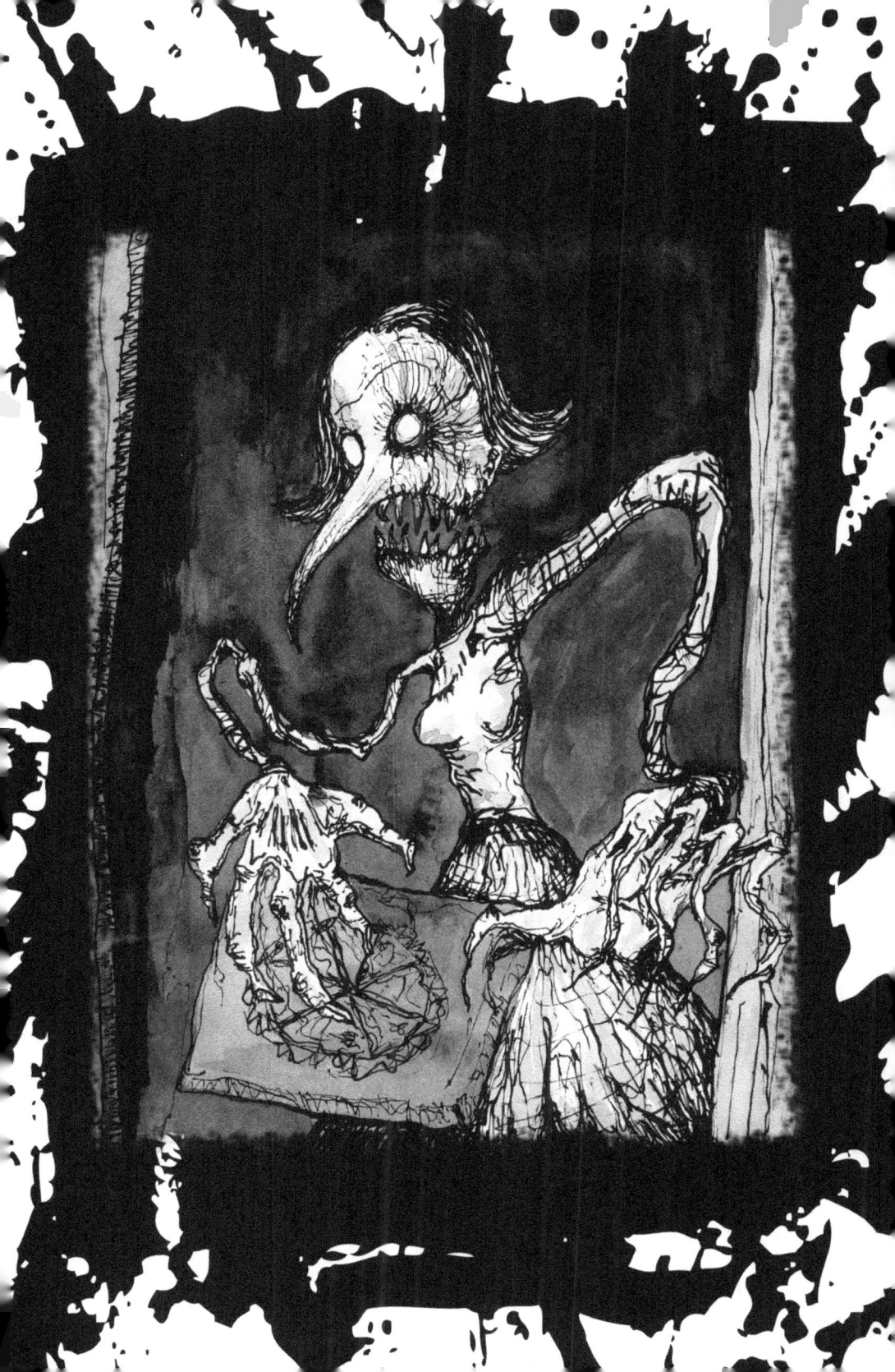

The smell of an old pond

Intruded in the garage of the cul-de-sac

Hung in a line

Along the spine of a fallen branch

Were the five drab colored fish

Their eyes staring vacantly at The Blob

Towering before me

A girth beyond physical description

And a smile crawled across its face

Larger than a premium rack of ribs

Peeling apart with the scent of gumbo and traditional jazz

Both scents embraced

Painting a portrait of the bayou

And the sea of the street pulled me back

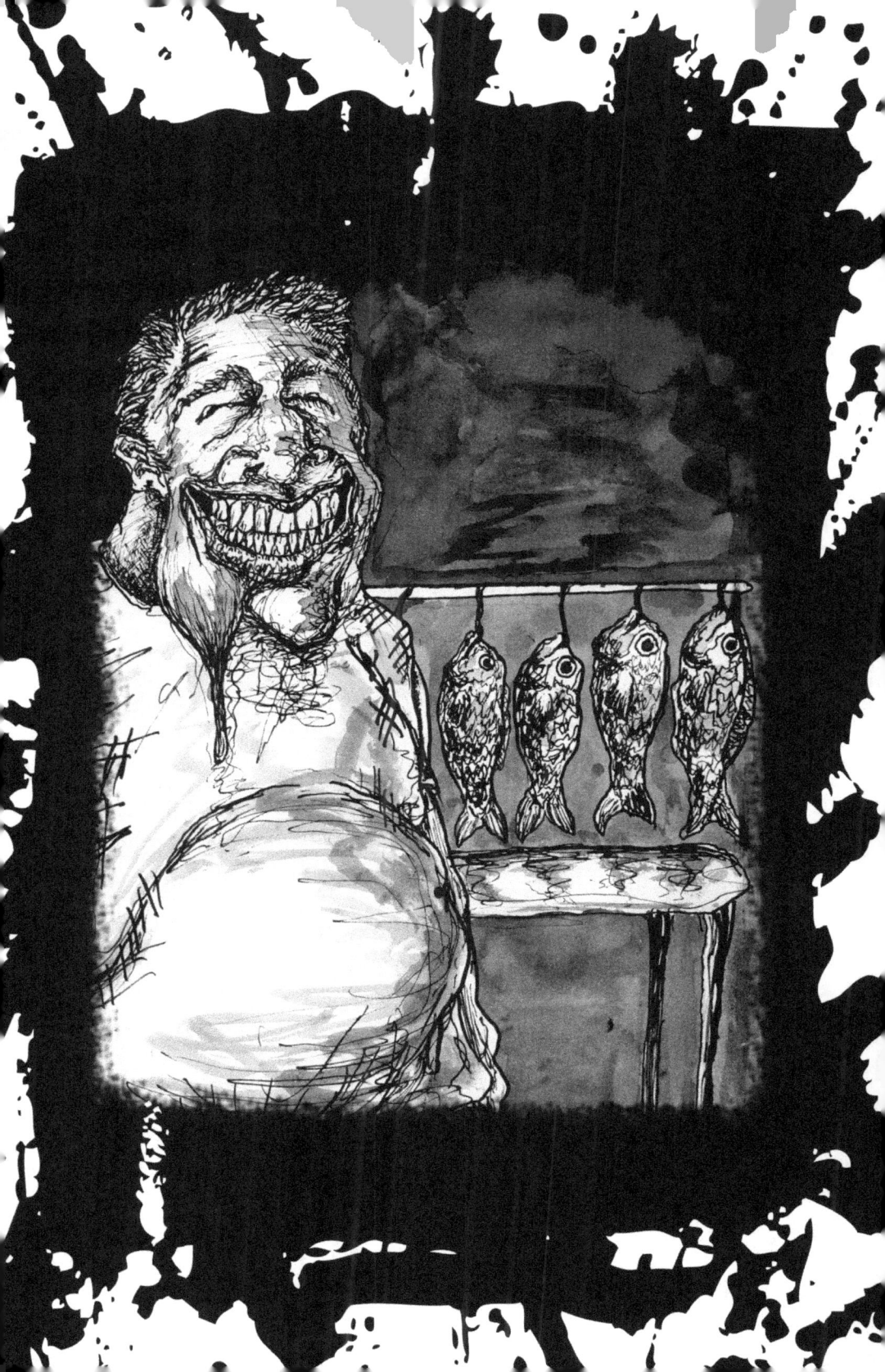

The wailing tore

Open the door

Confronted with two small women

And a screaming maw

Intelligible words

Pulled from unintelligible masses of sound

Informed of ghosts and imminent danger

While the two women giggled

Free from worry of such phantasms

Condemning the jaws

Of such foolish fantasies

While an employed babysitter

Seemed a fictitious fabrication

Sly smiles and thinly disguised wiles,

Beaded pigtails and painted nails,

Guided me from the horrors

Happening inside

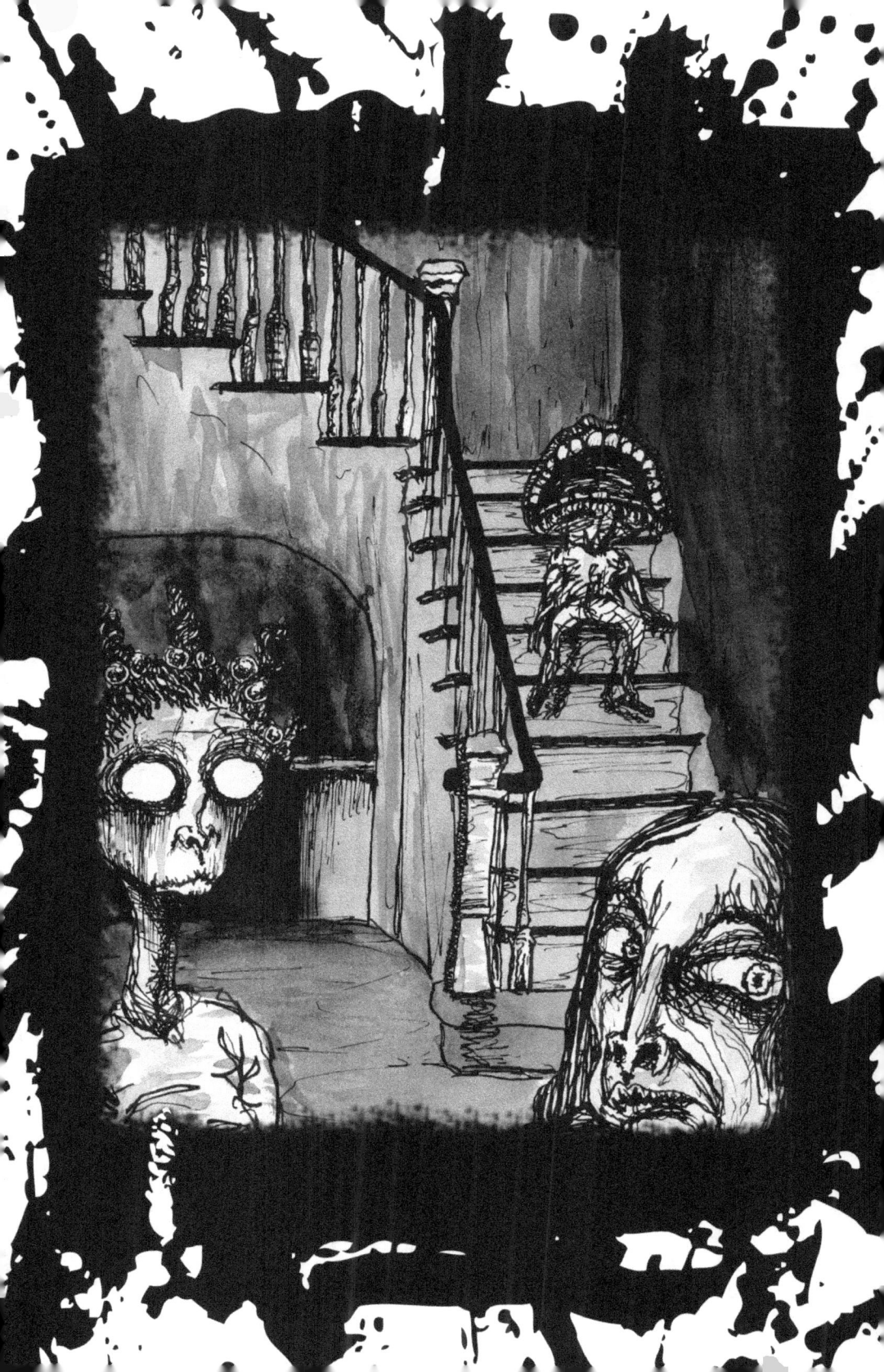

Metal infantry

Planted in the tortured soil

Around the hastily assembled compound.

A greenhouse in the desert,

Abandoned halfway built,

Due to the absurdity of the project.

The statues in the lawn

Variations on Frankenstein's monster

If he had raided scrap heaps

Instead of graveyards.

Only a gnome could inhabit

This maze of refuse/

And surely did a gnome appear at the door

Looking a little confused

Standing a hair taller

Than the tool bench in the entryway

His servants gently moaned with the wind

As if to facilitate my safe exit

From his humble home

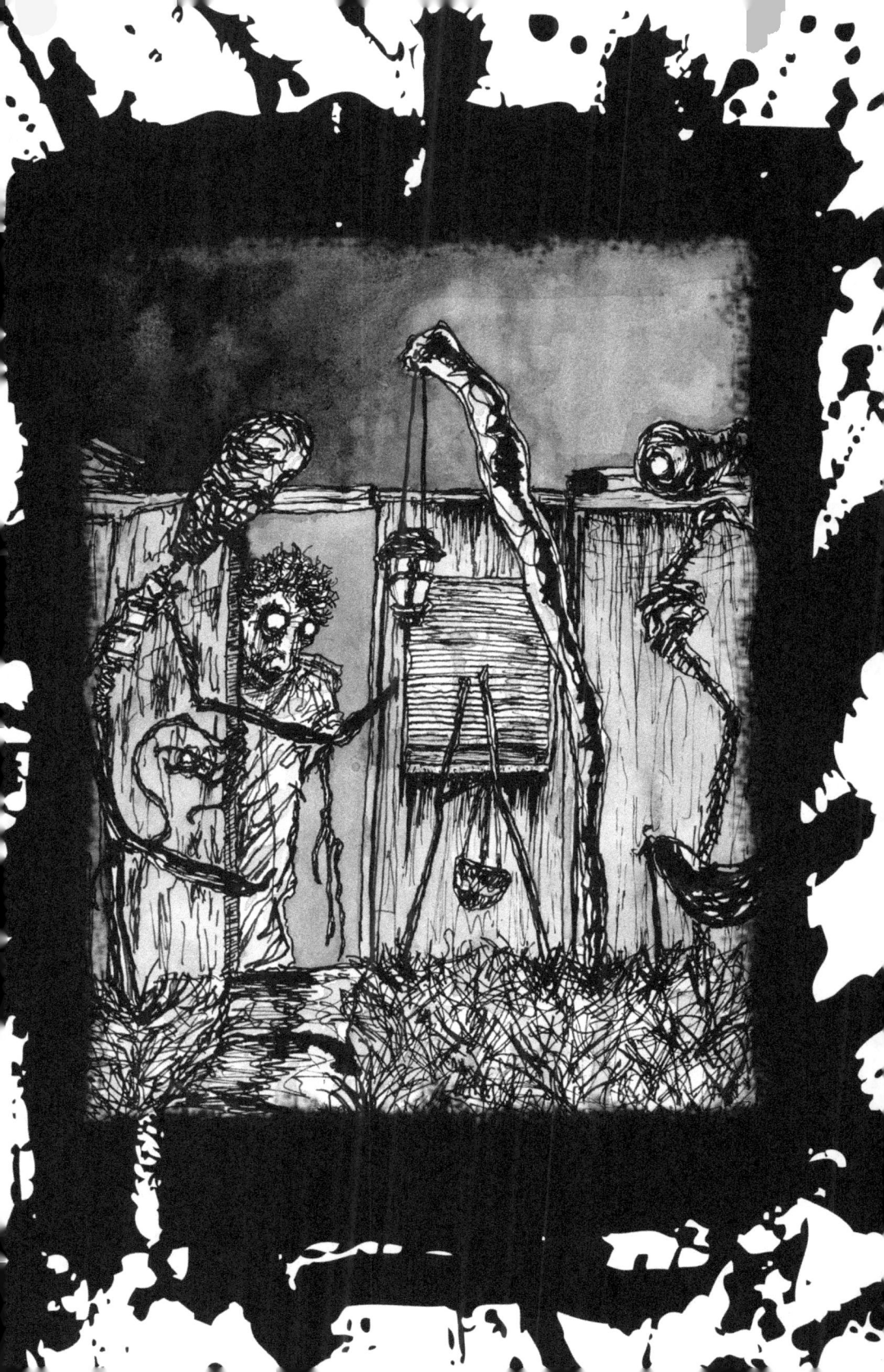

Country Club Road

The most literally named street in all of Bloomington

Kissed the immaculately kept green of a golf course

Each house resembling the palace of a drug lord

Tasting the excess of success

As I arrived, the sky frowned

Beginning its ejaculation over the well trimmed grass

The slow trek towards the architectural behemoth

Interrupted by a flash of light with each step

Transported me to the set of a B horror movie

My death march accompanied by the
falling rain

Egging me on to some dismal fate

As if some failure of human logic awaited me within

The doorbell chimed cheerfully

Shattering the spooky spell

And a teenager walked out

His face like glass

Too smooth, too frightened to be a killer

Not on Country Club Road

Not by the golf course

Not in Bloomington

Down the slender tarmac earthworm

Lit by the wolf's monthly bane

To Downs, IL

Far away from the scent of the ovens

As I wafted through the country

Over the corn and pebbles

"It's a mansion, you can't miss it"

Echoed the words of Kirsten

Flying into the emptiness of the cold night

Until a castle is assembled

By the glow of questing headlights

As the grass parted

Like the rubber red sea

A jeep calmly rolled from the distant structure

Blocking the thin ropey path

I guess I couldn't be trusted to find my way

Through the darkness and swaying grass

A thin, wispy woman popped out

Leaning in through the window

Wide eyes dully illuminated

As a crispy slip of paper

Slid from her hand to mine

As she vanished

Past the road sign

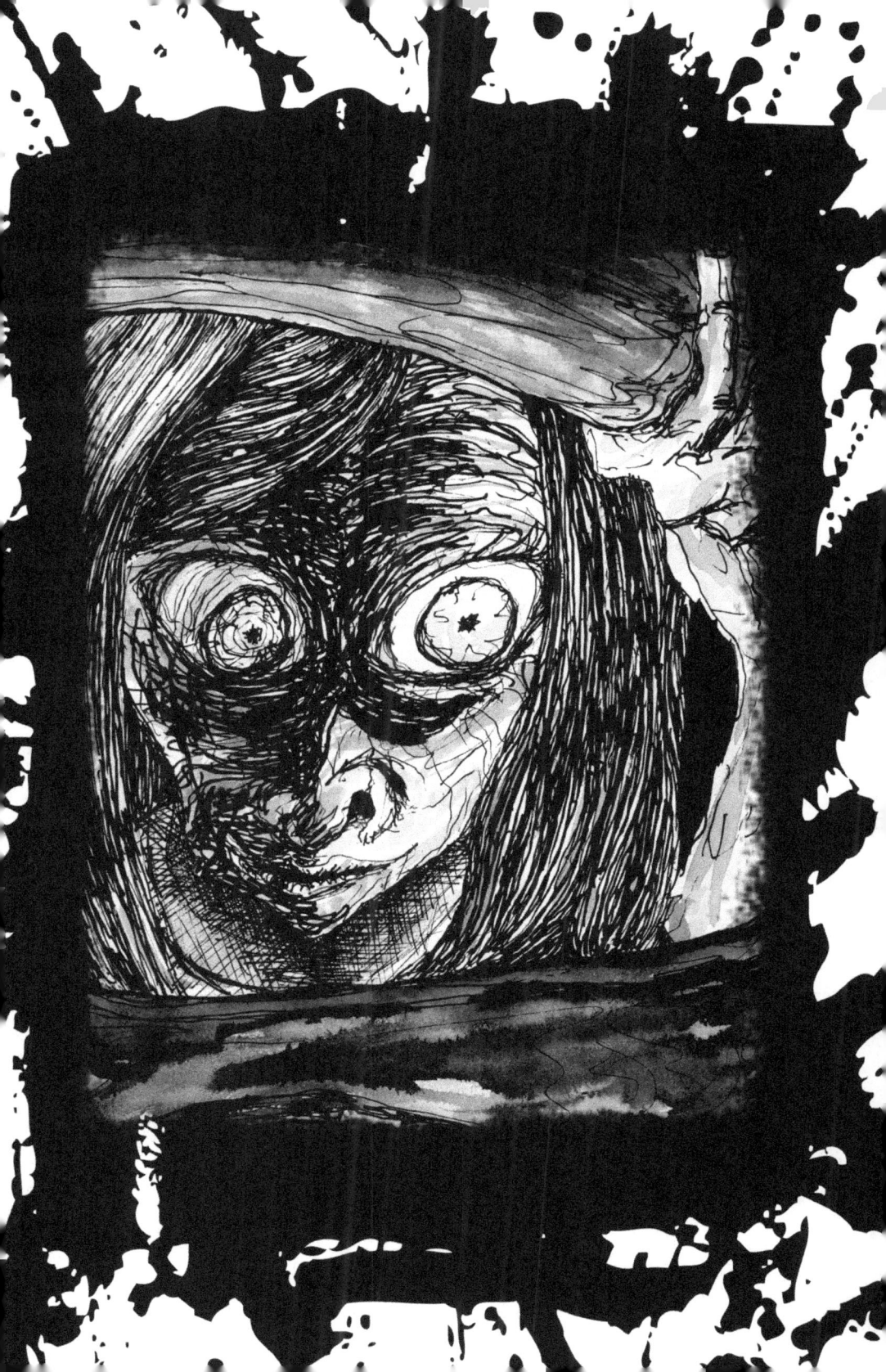

III. HOTELS

One room, infinite possibilities

The Chateau chattered

In a massive throb

Full of slobbering, staggering reptiles

The air alive with reptilian roars

As I circled the lobby

Bathed in the golden sepia filter of celebration

A tan clad man, suit akimbo

Underbite frothing

Full of blatant belligerence

His shoulders shuddered

As a woman standing to my right

Lifted one finger

Stroking my mustache

With a surrealistic intensity

And the man drew up, darkening my face

Eye lolling slightly to the left

"I will fuck you up, man"

His teeth rubbed the edge of his upper lip

Until the darkness of his face crept away

His hand fell to my shoulder

And snuck a grin

"I love ya, man"

Giggles surrounded me

From the two women, eyes glazed over

By the fog of luxury

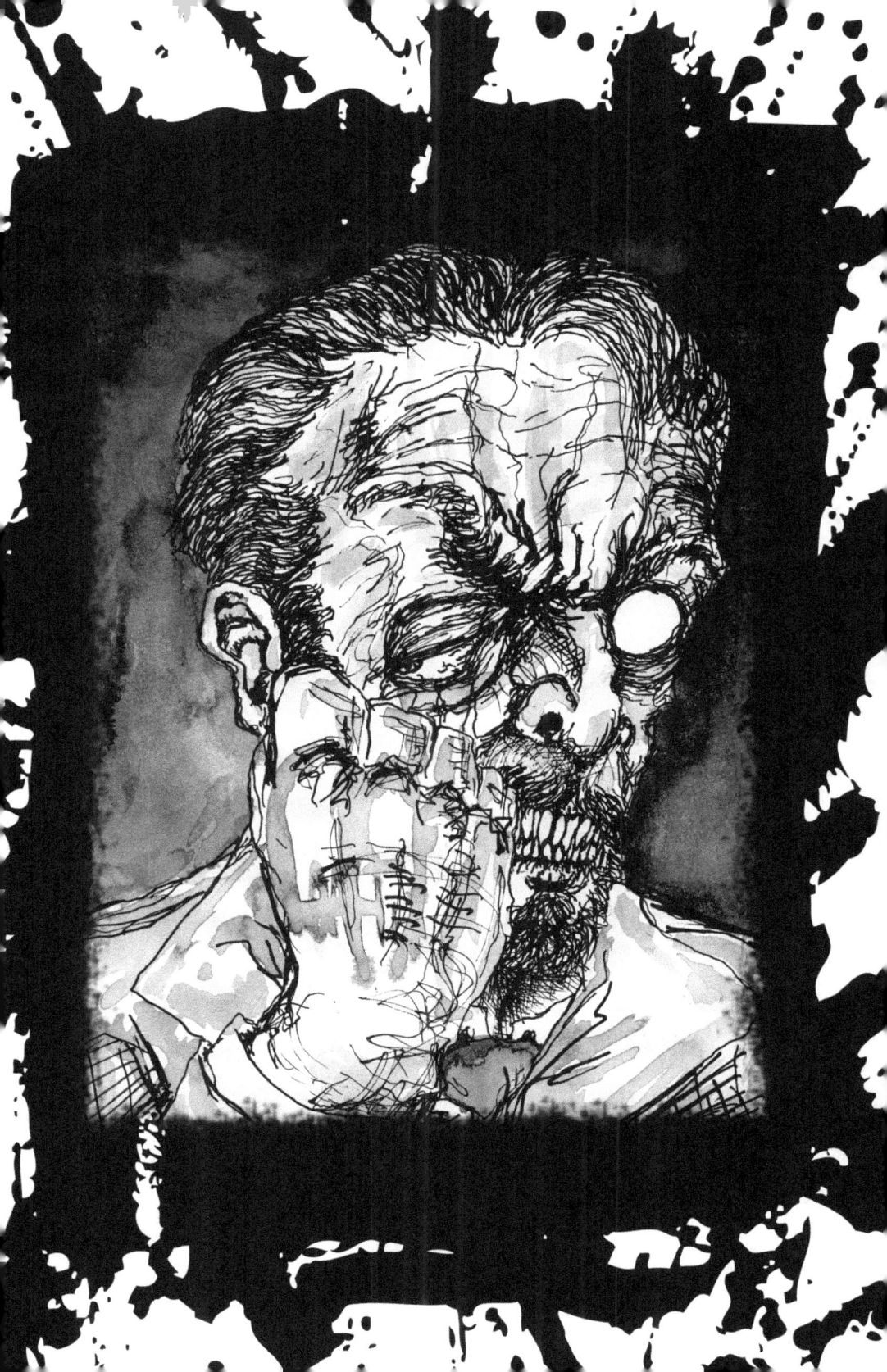

It was late

An easily navigable labyrinth

Was child's play

Minus a Minotaur

Past hundreds of rooms

Each as identical as the last

Simple, yet lengthy

As the monotony dragged on

STOP

A door on the left slightly ajar

Vomiting the dull hotel light

Of fixtures barely paid for

A man cast in the role of a stereotypical pedophile

Stood without pants in the fluorescent light

The dangling of his dick

Pretended to fit in

With the mundane surroundings

Of those a little bit better off

But only a little bit

His eyes scurried like scarabs

As I walked past

But his shame never came

He never moved

He just stayed the same

"C'mon, chug a beer with us?"

Veiny claws grasped a metallic blue can of Bud Light

Connected to a short, humped woman

The room was arranged by drunken hands

Shirts strewn about

Defeated duds

Collars contorted in deflated screams

I took the beer

Coerced by the woman's insistent grin

And brought it to my lips

Letting a small drip

Trickle through my ivory gates

Much to the excitement of the two

Seems I was off the hook

The can became my companion

For the walk down to the car

And finally parted ways

In the maw of the trash can

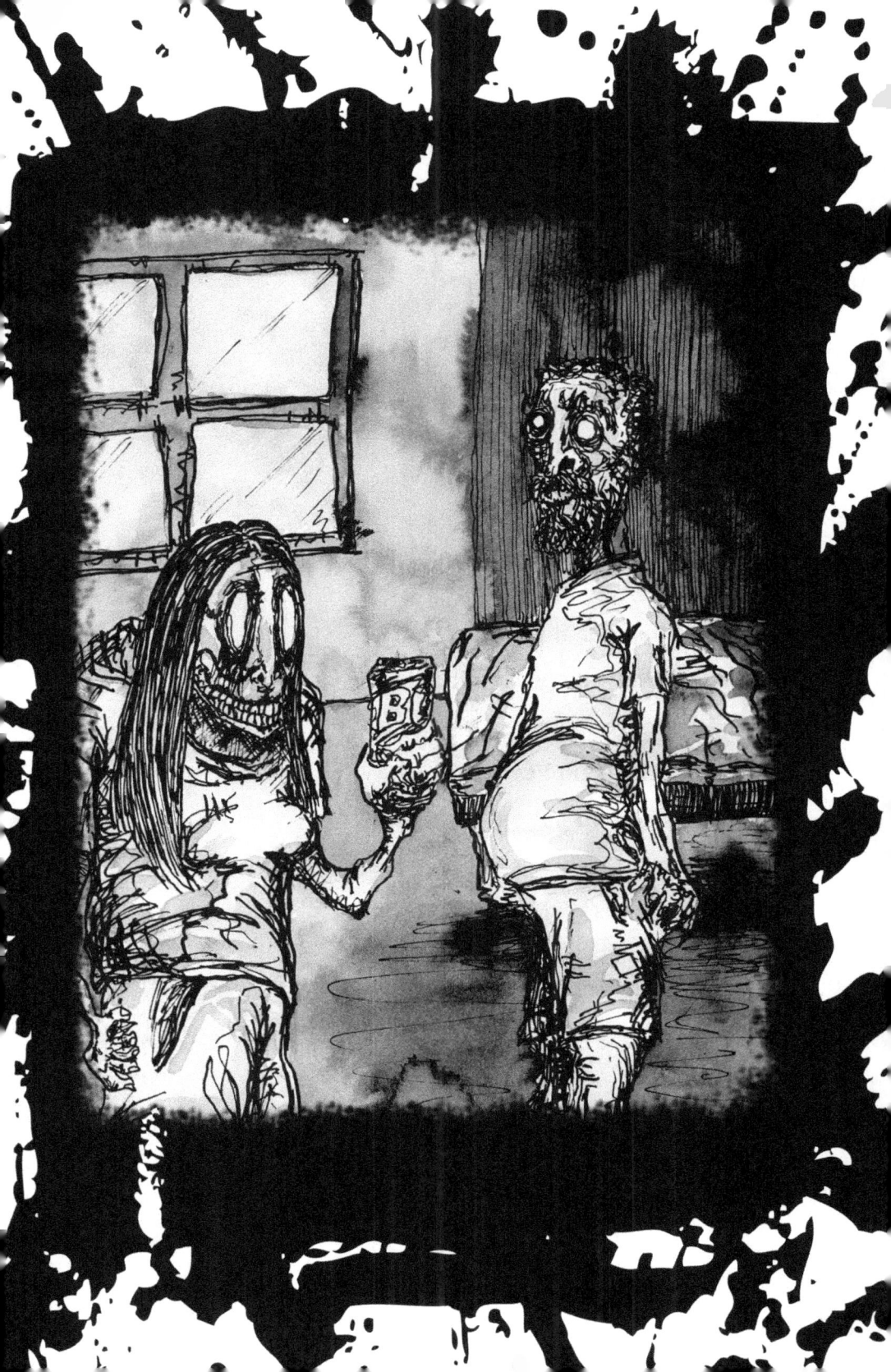

A phone call

"Do you guys have underwear toppings?"

"We're fresh out"

Drunken laughter drowned out rational response

And the night slid with grease

To Eastland Suites

Built like a dry bayou

Room 115 cavorted with cackling

Set on crackling

With the inebriated grins

Of a bloodthirsty beast

"Oh, you here for the gangbang?"

Sputtered a lump on the sofa

As girlish giggles galloped around the corner

As the laughter continued

In spite of societal implications

That masculine domination

Almost always

Has evil intentions

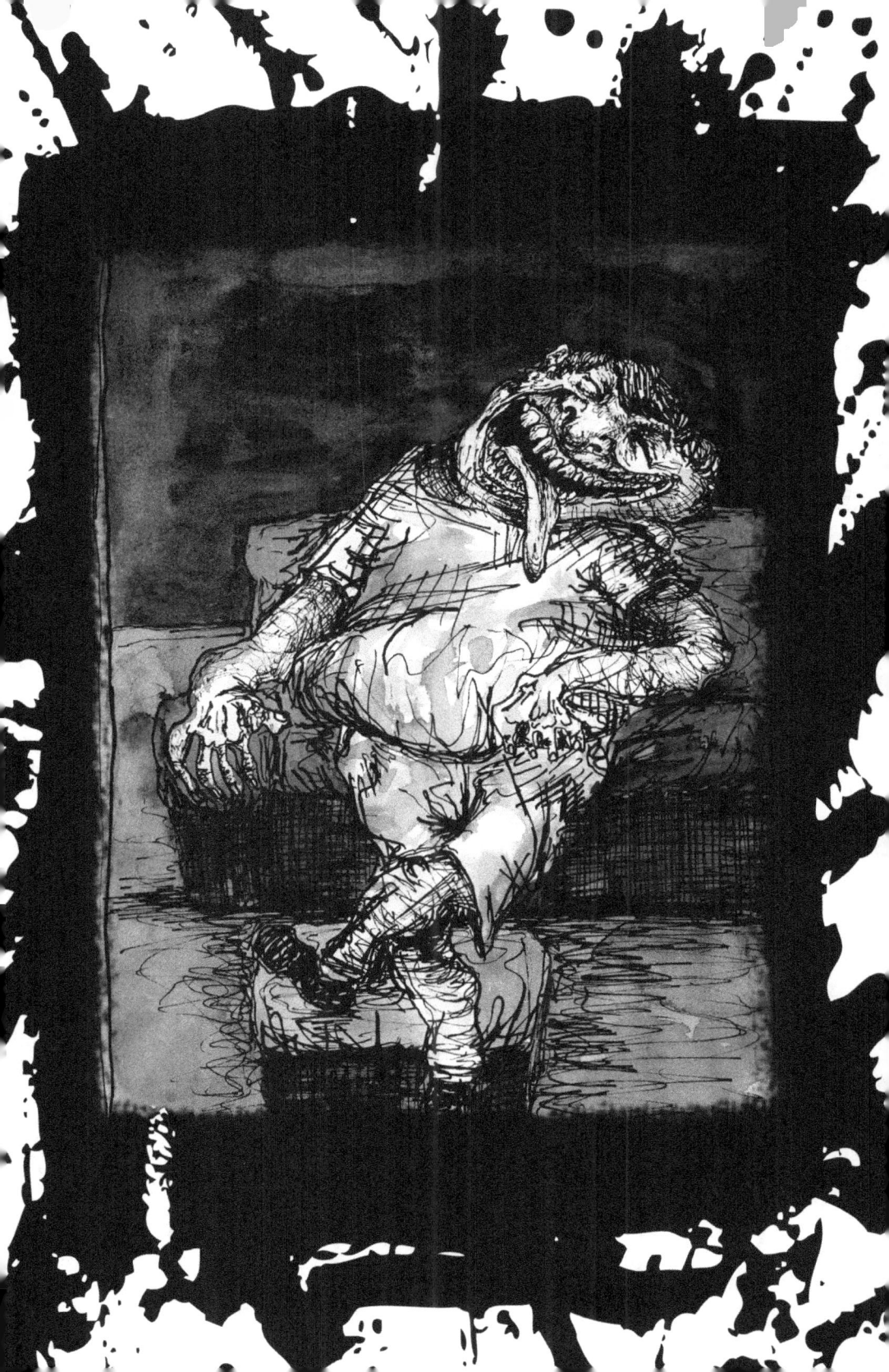

A hotel room

Is like a grab bag

At a toddler's party

You could get nothing

Or you could get something so strange

There would be no explanation that would satisfy

Answered the door

A woman old and frazzled

Head adorned with a red bandanna

Serving as sentry

For another bedded woman

Who lay without pants

In a bed clearly designed for two

I was ordered to appear here

But I did not seem invited

As dead eyes seemed to suggest

Okay, whatever, I'm just the pizza man

I'll get out of your hair

I don't care

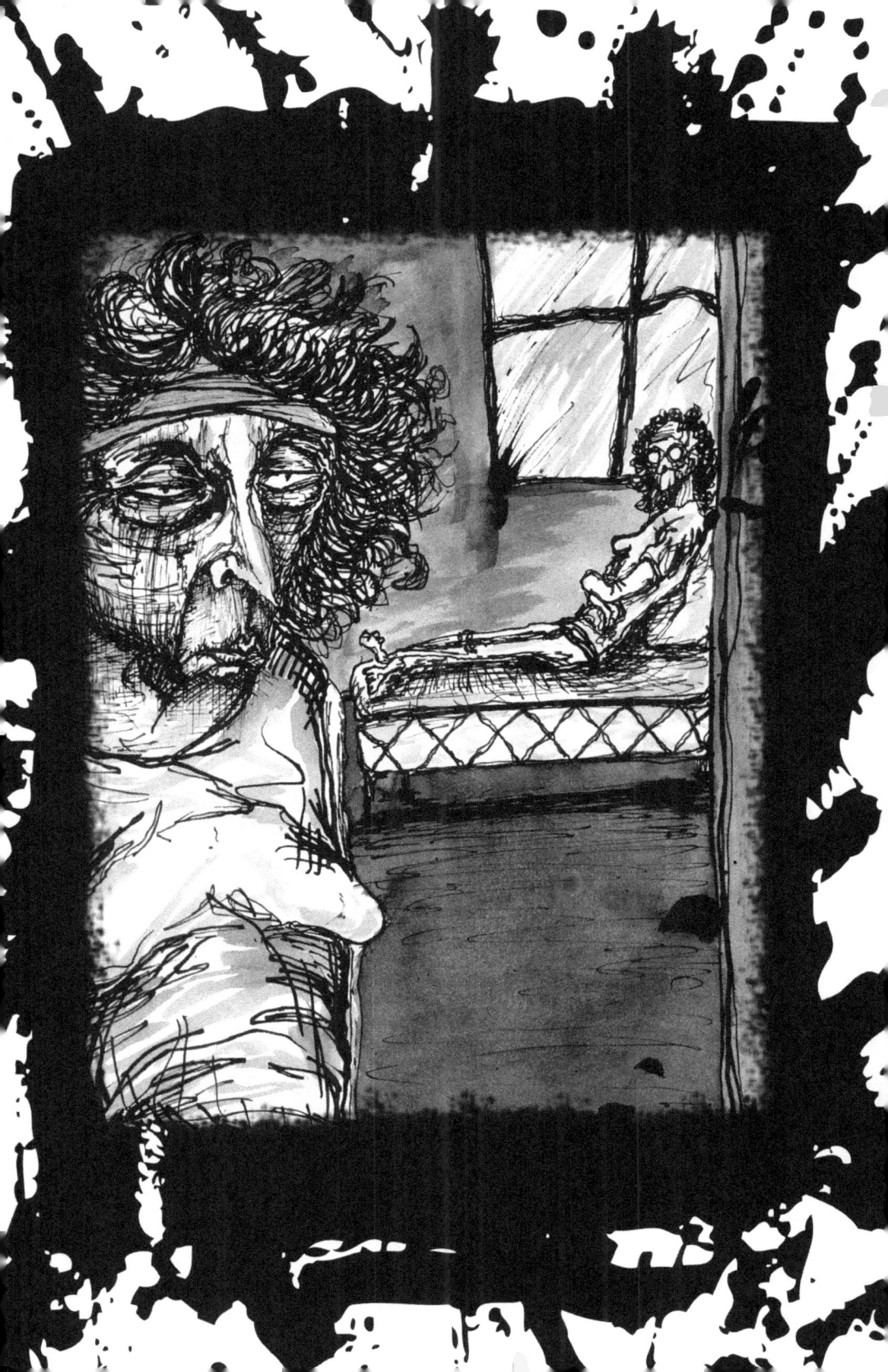

Up

Up

Up

Up

UP

His face was the contorted wasteland of a graveyard

Lit by the moons of dismay

Was my presence reminiscent of a past trauma?

Did I carry some fucked spirit

Encircled by the wings of Satan?

Had I suddenly transformed into a group of fauna?

His movements were subtle

Framed by a cautious energy

As he shrunk slowly in size

Flanked by a familial female

Eyes fixed in permanent vacancy

They had both swam

But in a chemical vat?

The juxtaposition of their faces

Seemed indicative that

Something foul had gone on

The elevator doors opened

And all which was wrong

Was suddenly wiped away

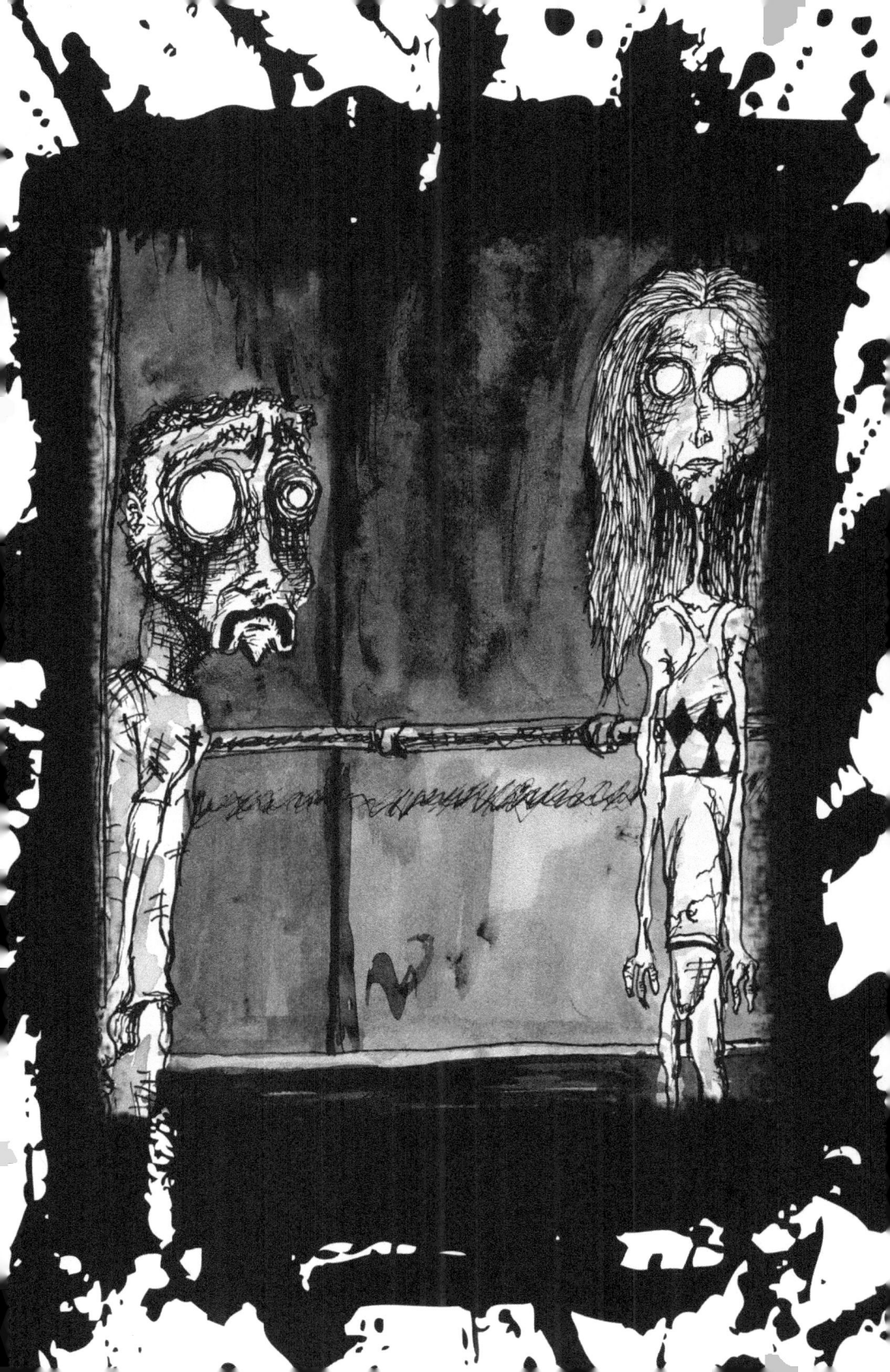

The bastard twin of the Chateau

Lay decaying on Rust Road

Its pillars sagging

Its facade moaning

Under the weight of neglect

The front entrance

Its fashionable maw

Like a first person mystery game

Both doors refused my efforts

Archaic pearlescent buttons lined the wall

Accompanied by faded names

Upon the depression, the door agreed

And a labyrinth of white beckoned from within

Clones of myself walked beside me

Through the silent corridors

As the minute sounds of footsteps

Danced off the walls

Until interrupted by a timid shout

"Hey"

Across the hall

Leaning out of a square of dark

A shabbily dressed woman

The only human

Leftover from a time of grandeur

Oily pizza now in hand

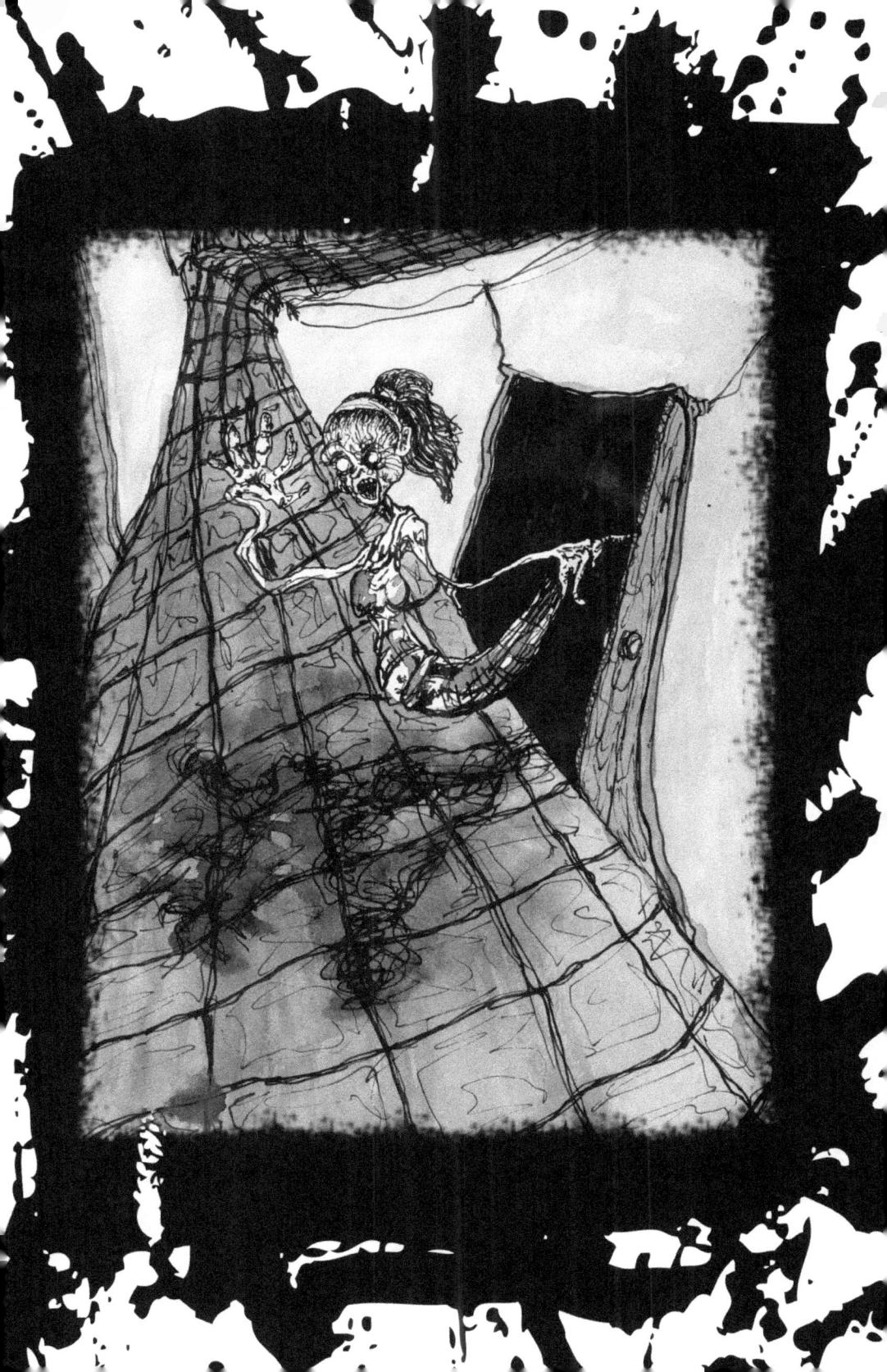

IV. WHEREVER ELSE

From competing pizza chains to retirement homes

A bleak day, driving for the Normal store

Short on drivers

Even shorter on a clue

The receipt ushered me to the heart of downtown

As Domino's came into view

GPS shrieked and vanished

Confusion took me by the belt

Into the brightly painted den

Of primitive pizza panderers

And was assaulted by the exuberant boom of a Domino's man

Who seemed cheerfully oblivious of his own
blatant betrayal

Content to disappear into the colorful depths

And devour the carelessly tossed delicacy of the enemy

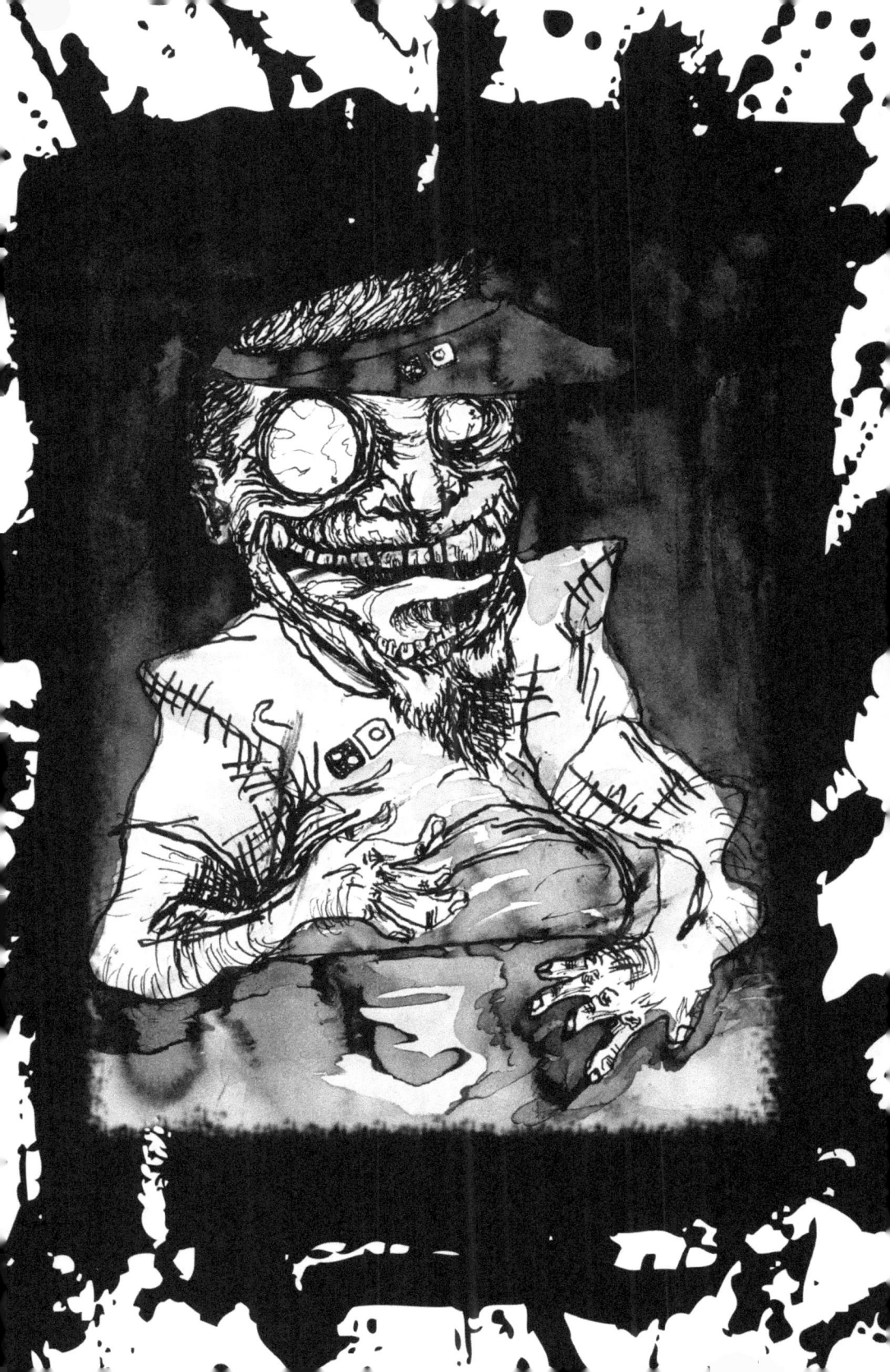

The sky was clear

Partially obscured

By the State Farm laboratory

Empty as the day shift at a strip club

Canvas above like Toy Story

And the air was still

Still blowing slightly

As my decaying phone snores a little

A flash of white glinted in the corner of my eye

Which belonged to a hanging tooth

Suspended from the abnormally vacant mouth

Of a small man

Whose head and hands were all to be seen

He remained silent throughout the transaction

A curious eye constantly affixed

As he disappeared around the corner

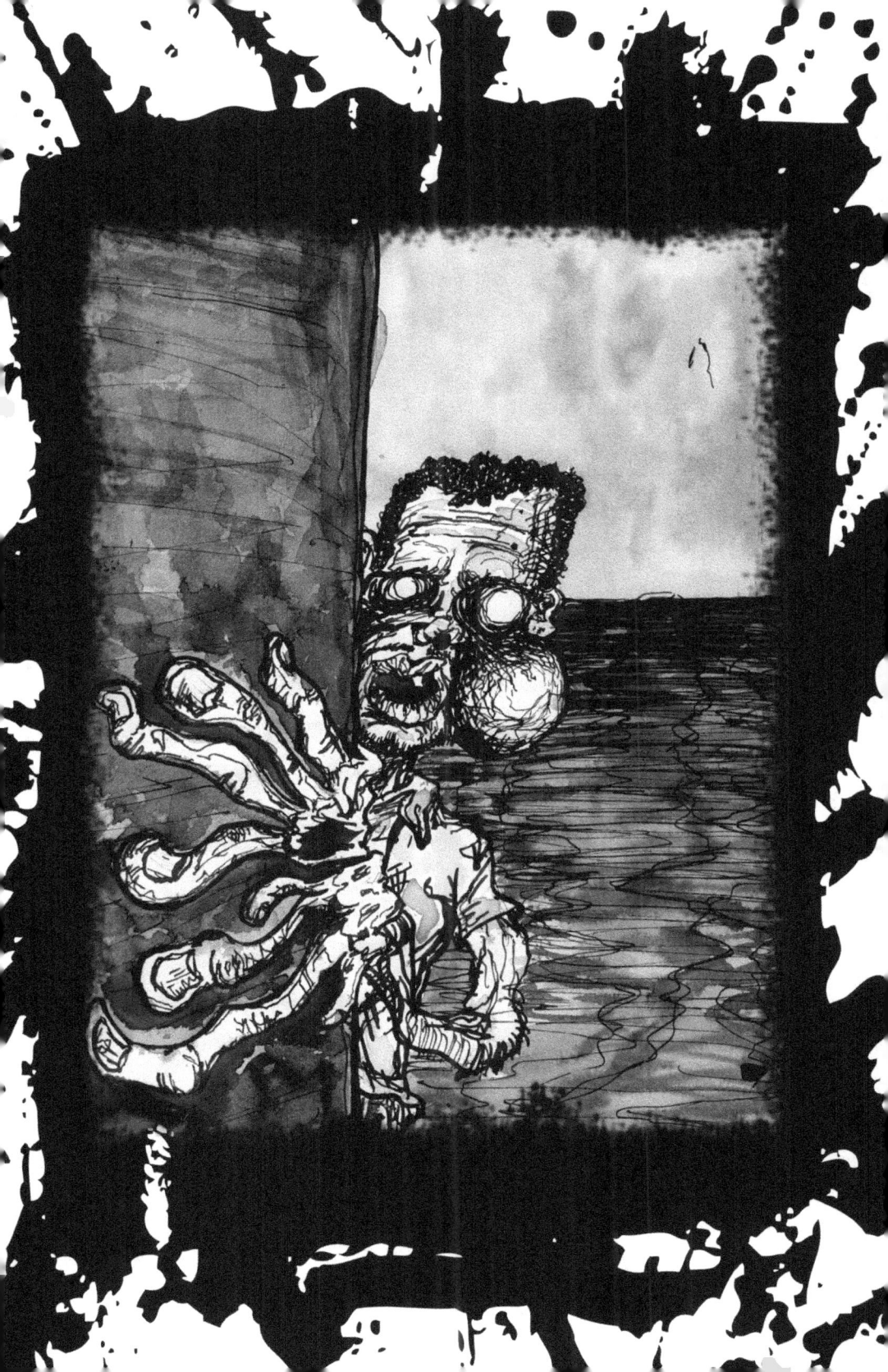

Abandoned

Except for a pair of security guards

And then

A bearded delivery driver

From Mugsy's pub

Comes and sits beside me

As I wait for Emily

Minimum wage comrades

Or at least a shared experience

Minutes pass by

Slowly vomiting into hours

Until a turnstile does a drunken twirl

And a slug-like man seeps through

With gnarled growths of bramble on his cheeks

......Emily?

This mucus coated man did not resemble my expectation

At all

But I suppose that's okay

He takes the pizza without pomp

As I leave I look back

The Mugsy's man was getting comfortable

I've been there, man

I've been there

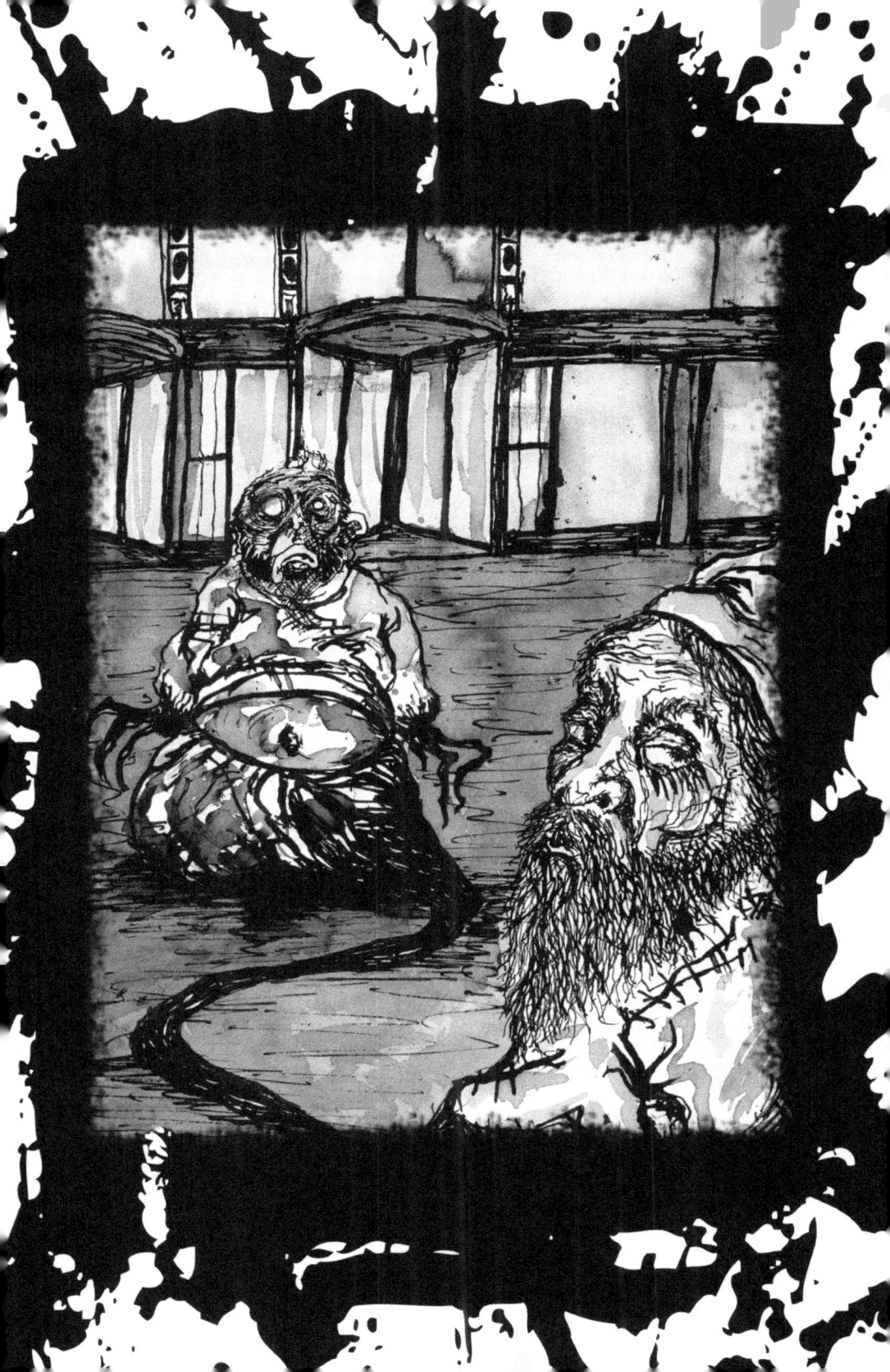

Nails and needles

Sometimes words do small justice

To the sounds they represent

Lackadaisical lawyers of syntax and sonics

Failed me again

The nail salon assaulted me with sick atmosphere

As a thin masked lady stood resplendently drab

 Over a seated and strapped patient

Her gaze shifted upwards

Confused of such a brightly colored, greased man

In her chamber littered with rusted chrome

Taking the pizza with a subtle suspicion

Her eyes chased me right out the door

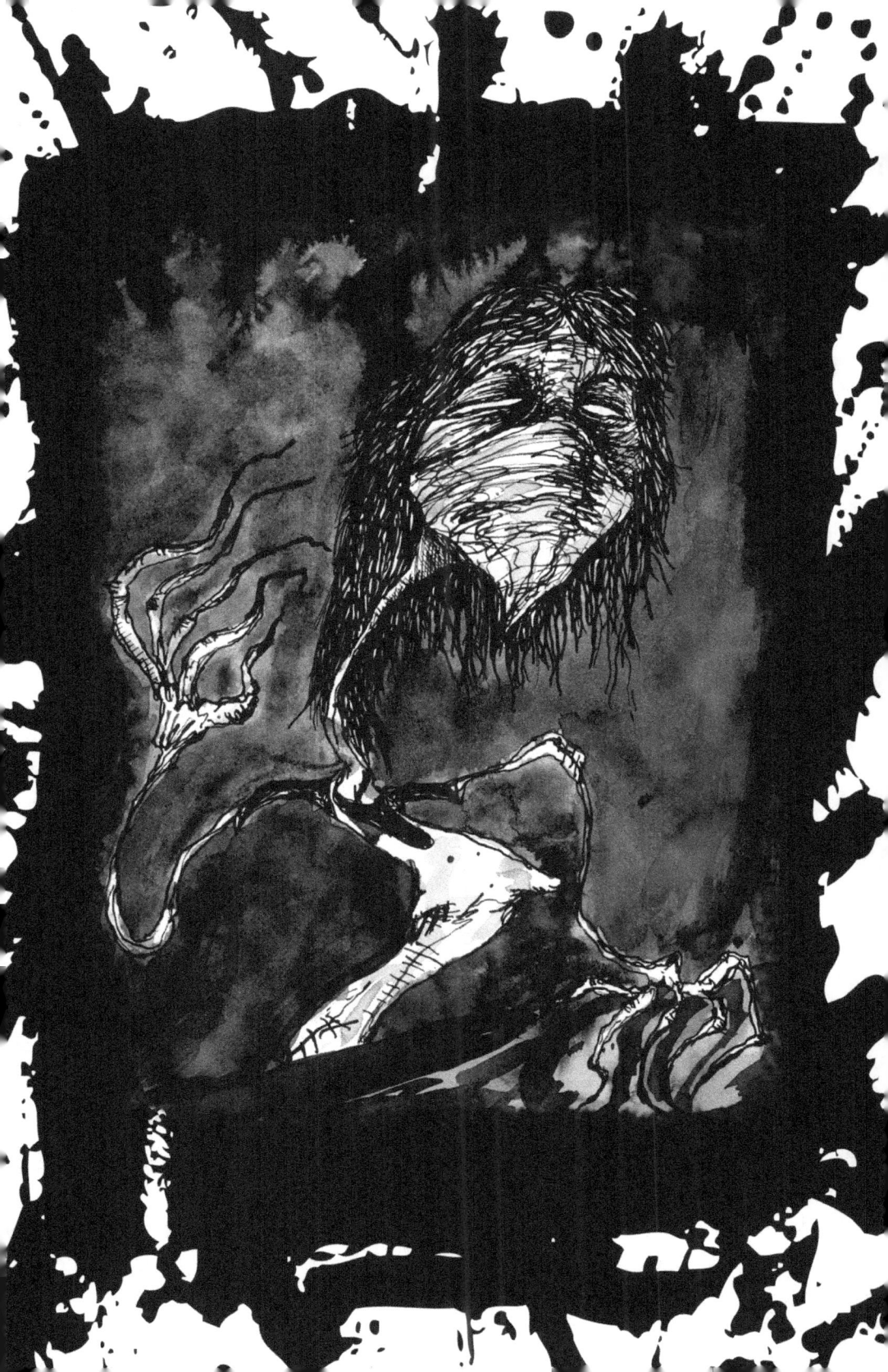

Retirement homes are always so immaculately kept,

Sharply juxtaposed by the crumbling state of their residents,

Halls a calmly insistent shade of white,

Floors covered in faded, bristling patterns.

The receipt remained silent on this one

A gnarled set of bones lay draped over a lime armchair

"Do you know who ordered a pizza?"

The words fell uselessly to the floor

Unable to penetrate the exterior of death

That seemed to cloud this woman

Head bent towards the floor

Like a street sign after a drunken drive by

The question seemed to suspend time

As the woman remained a twisted sculpture

Swaying slightly

As if enjoying a spring breeze

I moved on

One eye over my shoulder

Fixed on her zombified form

Until the corner hid her

From view

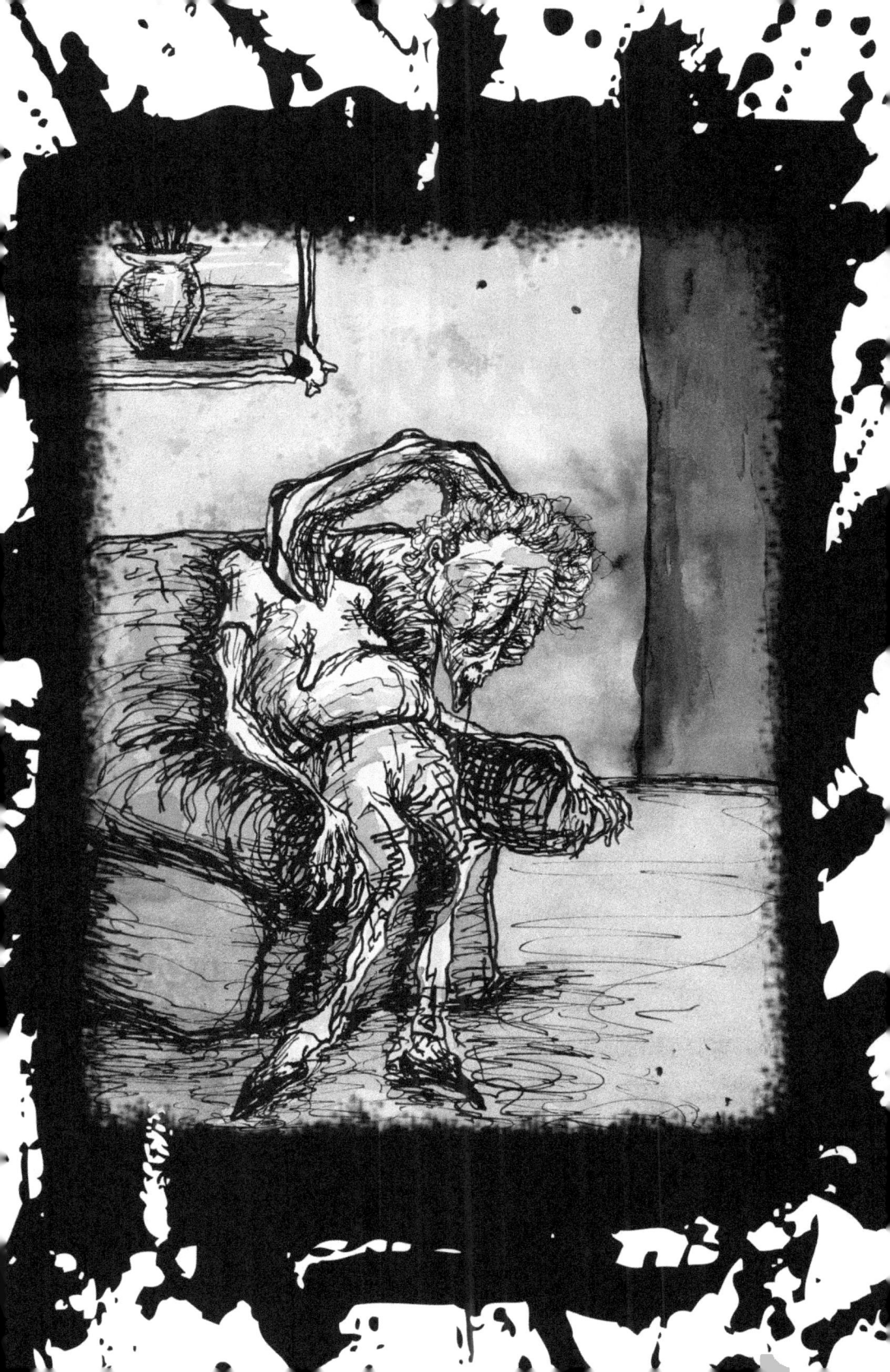

It was shaking

The small shack on the side of the road

Looking out at the barbed wire

Of what could easily be a testing facility

For all manner of nuclear hellfire

It was shaking

The shoulders of the shack threatened

To collapse under the sonic weight

Of Bollywood's deafening dance

A woman stood before me

Cloaked in color

Skin rippling with vibrations

Regurgitated by the black boxed banshees

Lining the room

Like an angry jury

Whose cries selfishly dominated the din

Words became useless

Words became

Useless

"Please sign here"

Vacant expression

Aural oppression

End of session

128

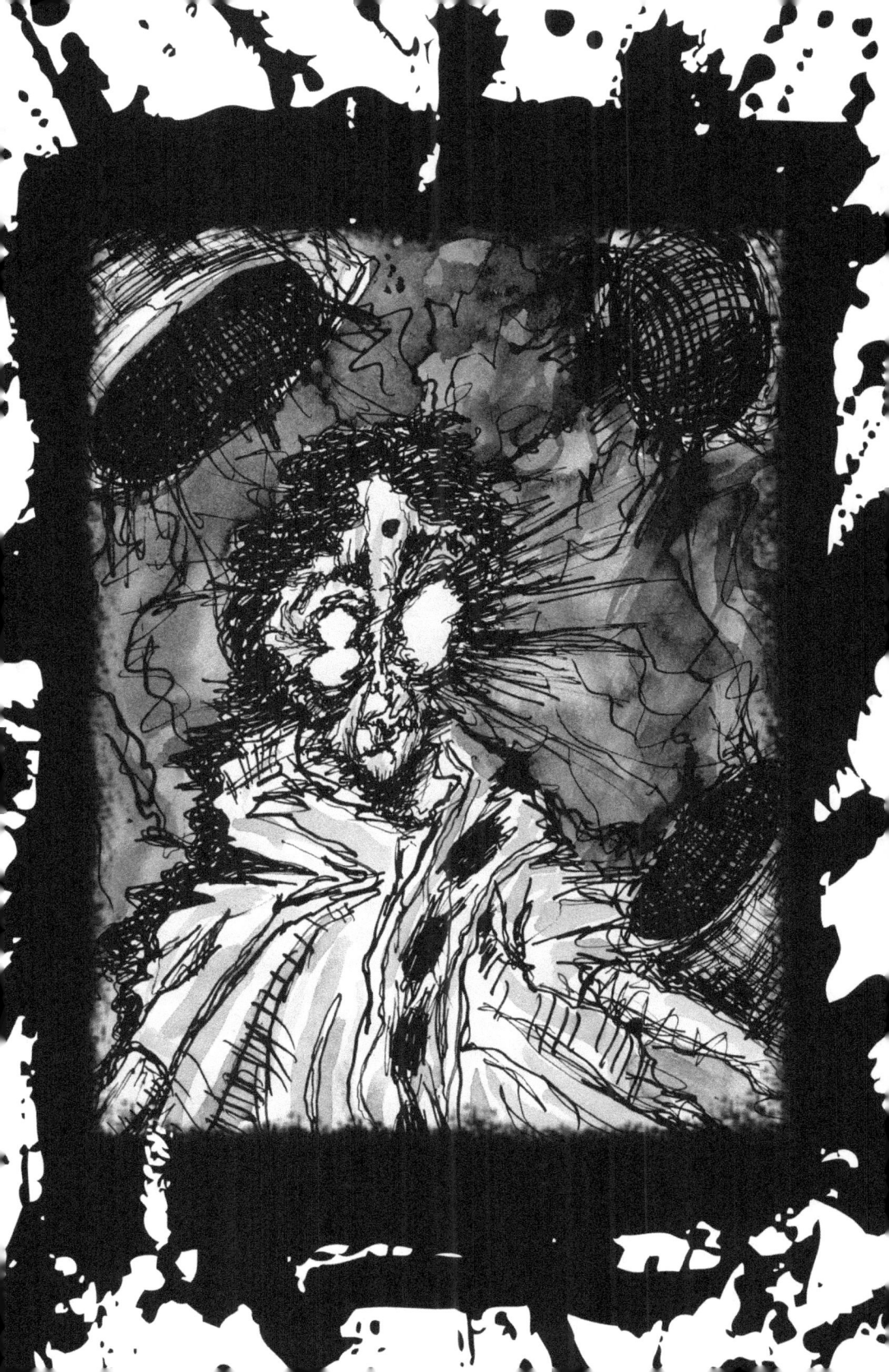

75 pizzas and a car full of shit

I couldn't do this alone

Destination outside of normal delivery range

To the Bloomington Center of Performing Arts

Shay followed, fading in an out

As steam attempted to obscure

My view of the road

And I was at the steps

In corporate red and khaki

An unexpected change from the tuxedos

Of orchestral concertos and oboe solos

Only now away from the stage

We filed in, pizzas soon becoming a wall

Of collapsible red and black

The ballroom was swarming

With feet and vocal chords

A man with a face like the utility wall of a tool shed

Let us finally free

With the quick flick of a wrist

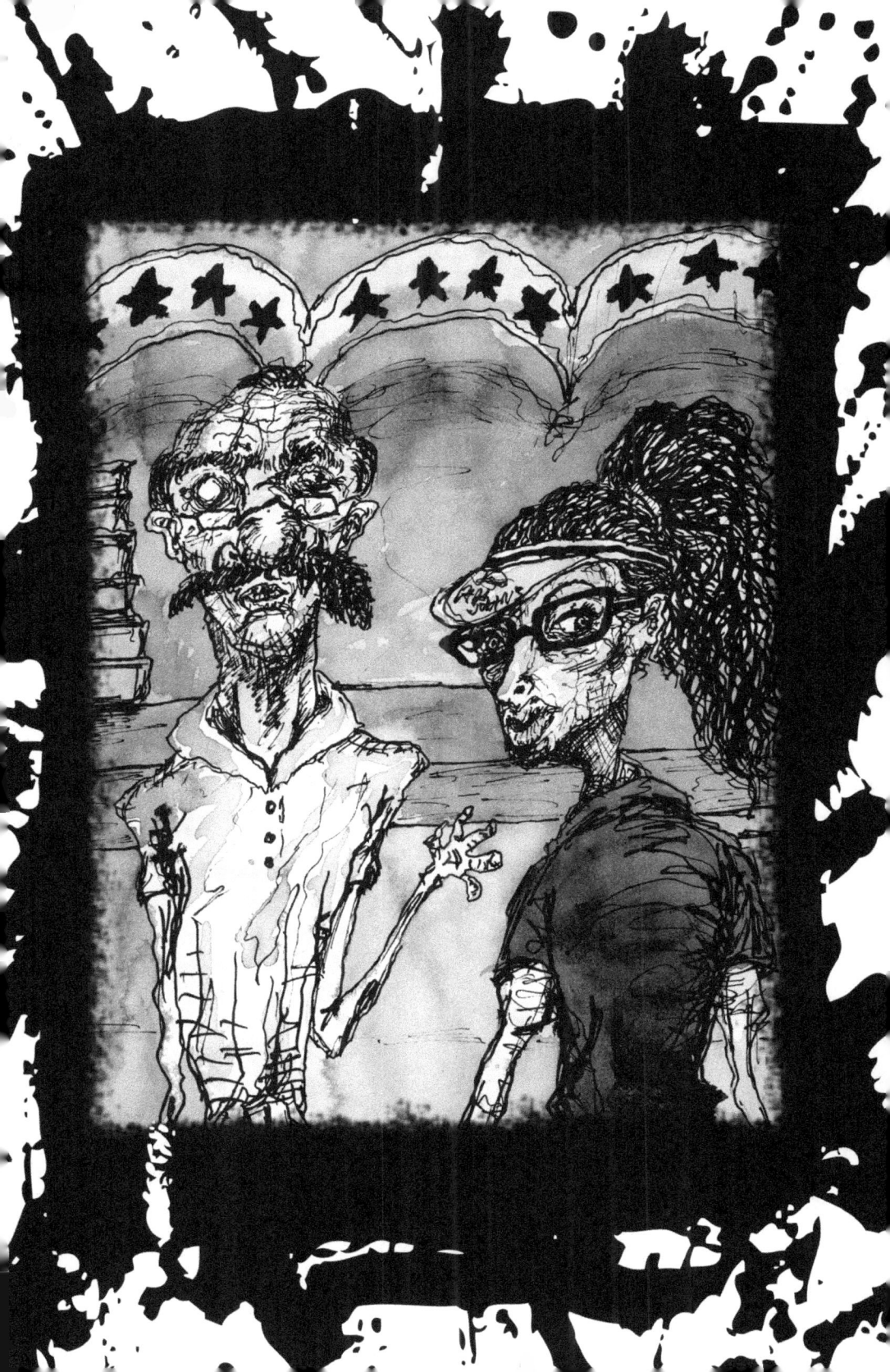

It crept up my neck towards my ears

Like the nostalgic nausea

Of that one time I filled the bathroom

With neon yellow vomit

Words of casual conviction

Uttered with a dispossessed drawl

But surely enough to placate

A brainwashed flock of sheep

Entrance subverted the sermon

Heads turned

As I placed my offerings on the table

The man standing before the sheep

Looked nothing like the vessel of God

Rather like an insurance salesman

After the realization that life is cruel

Has long since passed

Replaced by the passive hypnosis

Of preaching at the rec center

Two younger males put on their happy masks

Inquiring and poking

Into the life of some delivery boy

As if I have anything to tell them

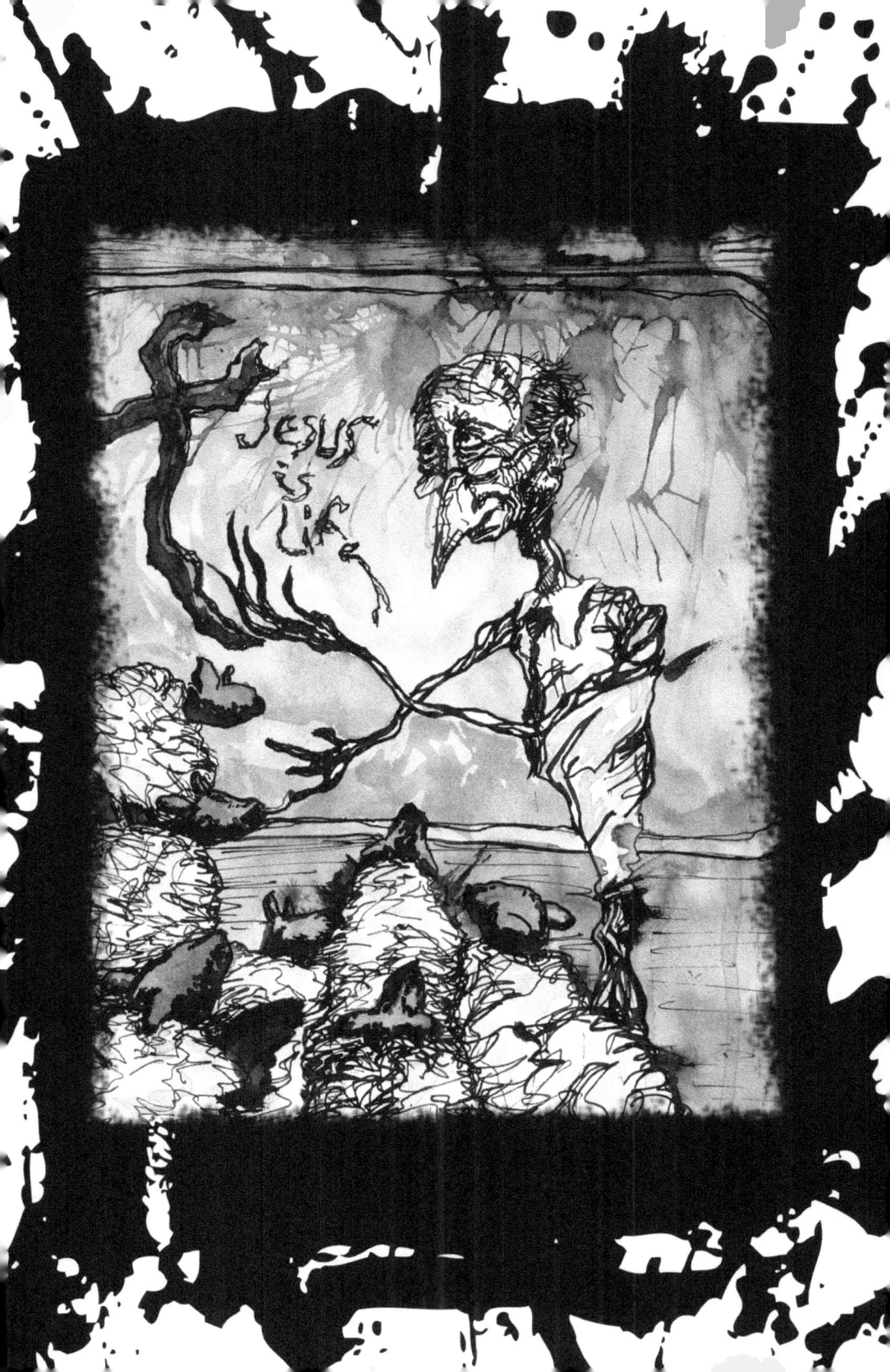

1615 East Empire Street

"This is the mall, right?"

Jason nodded

But at 9:34

The mall was closed

A futile tug at the door confirmed this

Just then

A man with a long broom walked just out of sight

Fuck

Back in the car, to the next door

The same man, just out of view again

A third trip around

Cleaning tables this time

Completely in view

Careful thuds on the door finally caught his ear

And pulled him towards the door

Wandering past the deserted storefronts

Job suspended by childlike wonder

Until Victoria's Secret seduced my gaze

Scantily clad mannequins imprisoned behind bars

Of temporary termination

A fleshy figure caught my inquiring eye

And the prison was dispelled

Returning to the land of lingerie

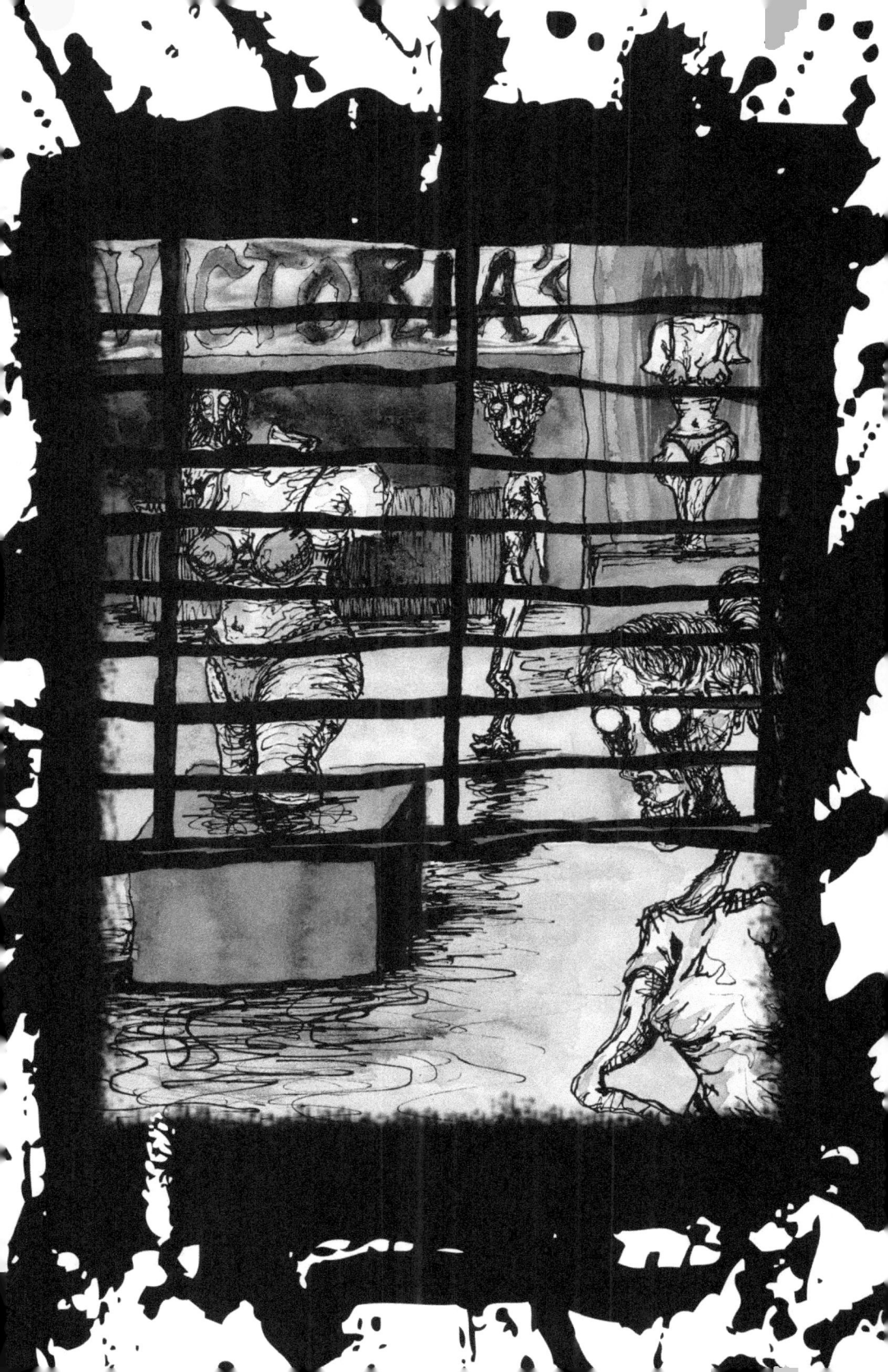

605 Pine Street

A battalion of domestic domiciles

Long since deprived of escape

From this desperate place

Receipt reads "blue trailer"

As if I am supposed to know where that is

Leering from down the line

Two blue trailers

Several knocks reveal a man

His hair a toasted prairie

In the event of the Mississippi burnings

His words a jumble of grunts and confused questions

His shirt stained and old

And his eyes buzzed around me

Like flies to filth

Mindless and without purpose

As he spoke, his mouth became

A line of wrecked cars

Falling into the deep crevasses of the earth

This was not the blue trailer

But what was?

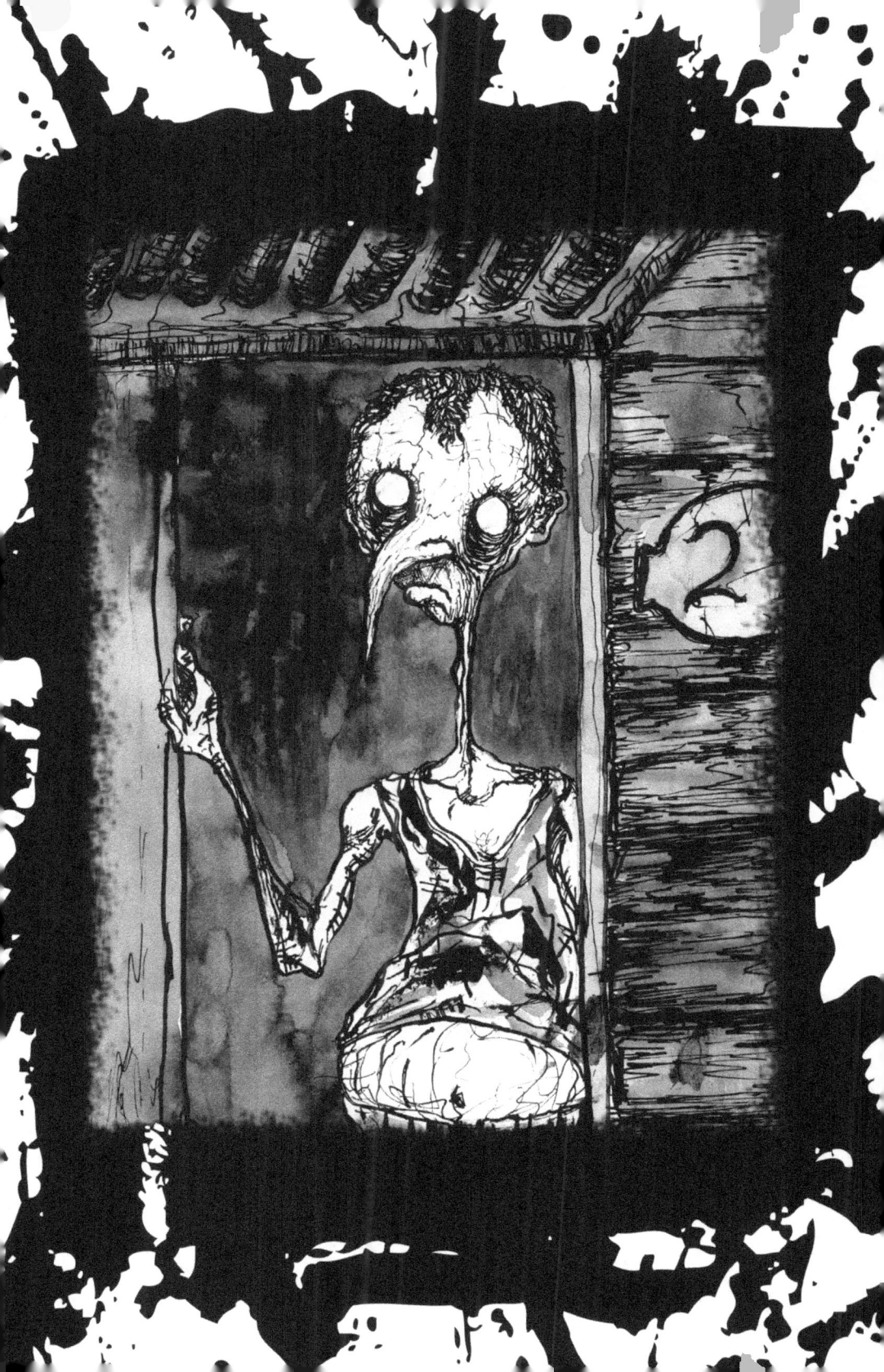

Flanked by trailers and lamps

The asphalt serpent uncoiled itself

Looking like something out of the Twilight Zone

As the rubber moans are suddenly stifled

And the trailer sleeps

Closer scrutiny uncovers nothing but suburban bones

And rusted apocalyptic memories

Are left to steep

In the cold coffee of neglect

Paint peeling and wood splitting

Feeling dead and gone

Countless phone calls

Bring no answers

As I am starting the car

A strangled shriek erupts from the void

And a shriveled car mechanic-looking motherfucker

Appears out of thin air, clutching the side of the car

Coming to claim his pizza

And as I drive away

Four notes echo through the air

As the man leaves me

With nothing but a blank stare

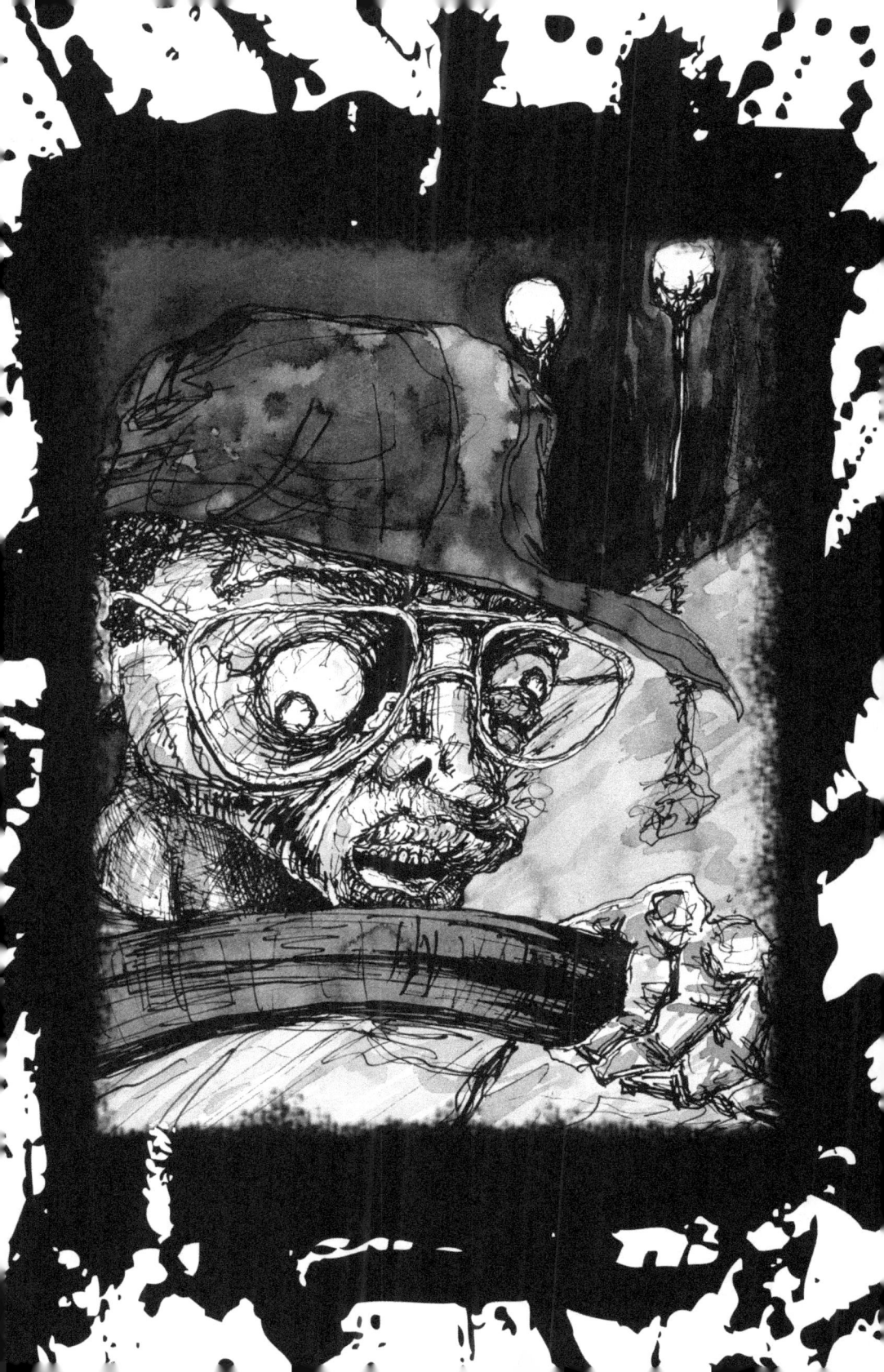

"MARI-HO!"

The cretinous crawl of a man

Burst through the glass door

Box of pineapple under arm

Responsible for the apocryphal accusations

Of a volatile environment

From behind horn rimmed glasses

Eyes squirmed like a duo of beetles

Reminded that his thin lipped snarl

Was the cause of the upheaval

Of all our schedules

And gave birth to late nights and overtime

Perpetrated a sort of legal, safe crime

Because of the lack of a lock

On his goblin growl

Long since expelled from the store

A ghostly apparition

Through rose colored retinas

Felt almost cinematic

On my final day

Of burnt hands

Dusted clothes

And the friends and foes

Made along the way

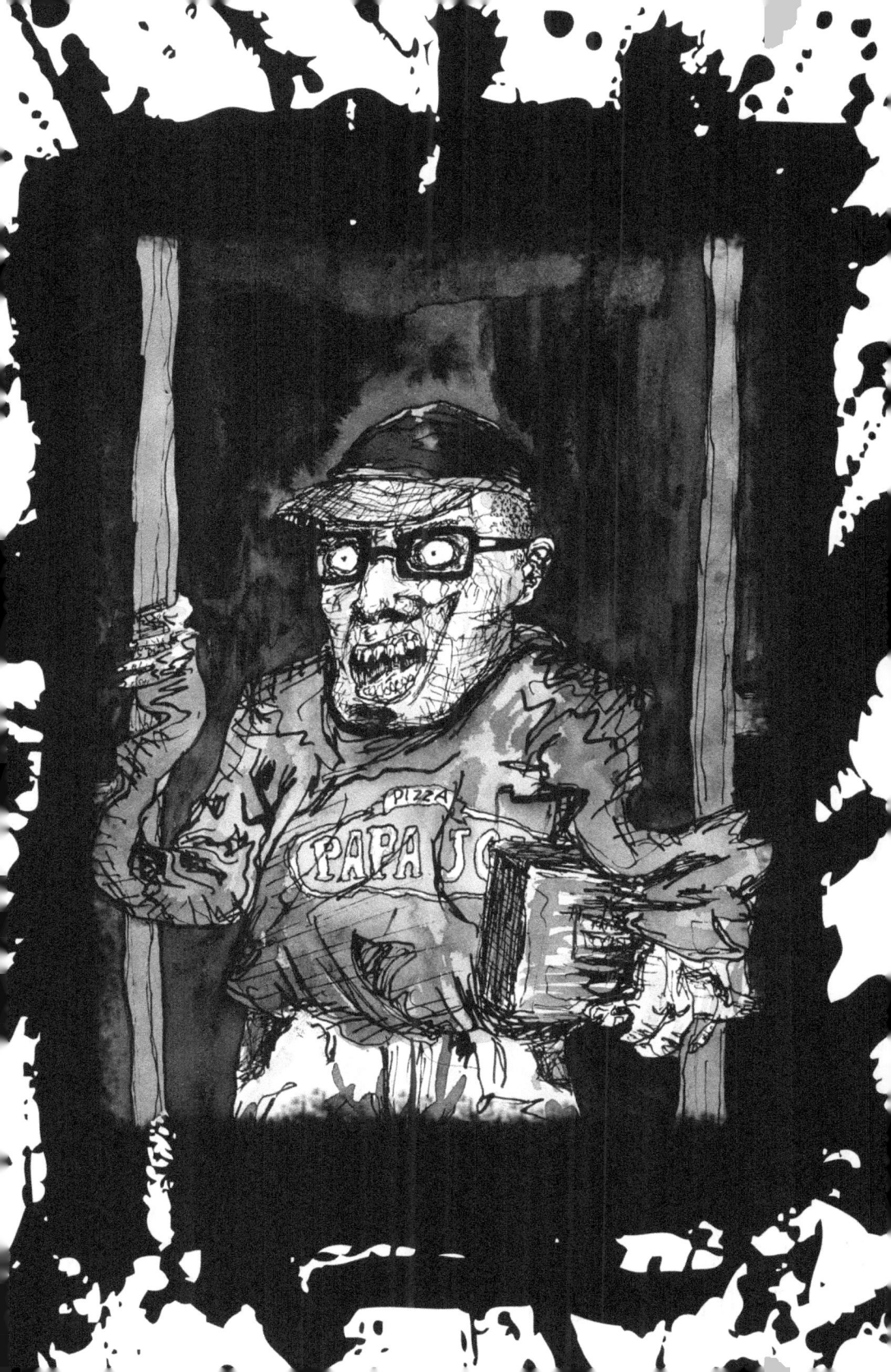